Challenging
Child
Protection

Research Highlights 57

RESEARCH HIGHLIGHTS IN SOCIAL WORK
This topical series examines areas of particular interest to those in social and community work and related fields. Each book draws together different aspects of the subject, highlighting relevant research and drawing out implications for policy and practice. The project is under the editorial direction of Professor Andrew Kendrick, Head of the School of Applied Social Sciences at the University of Strathclyde, Scotland.

other recent books in the series

Challenging Child Protection

New Directions in Safeguarding Children

Edited by Lorraine Waterhouse and Janice McGhee

Research Highlights 57

Jessica Kingsley *Publishers*
London and Philadelphia

Chapter 11 is abridged with permission from Wiley from the following article: Waterhouse, L. and McGee, J. (2013) 'Practitioner–mother relationships and the processes that bind them.' *Child and Family Social Work*. Article first published online, 30 April 2013, DOI: 10 1111/cfs.12074. © 2013 John Wiley & Sons LTD.

First published in 2015
by Jessica Kingsley Publishers
73 Collier Street
London N1 9BE, UK
and
400 Market Street, Suite 400
Philadelphia, PA 19106, USA

www.jkp.com

Library of Congress Cataloging in Publication Data
Challenging child protection : new directions in safeguarding children / edited by Lorraine Waterhouse and Janice McGhee.
    pages cm
  Includes bibliographical references and index.
  ISBN 978-1-84905-395-2 (alk. paper)
1. Child welfare. 2. Children--Services for. 3. Child abuse--Prevention. I. Waterhouse, Lorraine. II. McGhee, Janice.
  HV713.C3726 2015
  362.7--dc23
                     2015006633

British Library Cataloguing in Publication Data
A CIP catalogue record for this book is available from the British Library

ISBN 978 1 84905 395 2
eISBN 978 0 85700 760 5

Printed and bound in Great Britain

Contents

Part 3 Challenge Three: Working with Children and Families

Acknowledgements

We would like to acknowledge Professor Joyce Lishman for her advice in the early genesis of this volume, Professor Andrew Kendrick (series editor) for his continuing support and all the team at Jessica Kingsley Publishers.

Introduction
Challenging Child Protection and Safeguarding Children

Lorraine Waterhouse and Janice McGhee

This book strives to be anti-conventional, to stand back from our time, not for the sake of it, but to listen more acutely to individual authors from very different research backgrounds – both disciplinary and place. The intent is to develop an enriched conception of what is at stake in child protection and to resist for this purpose its almost compelling power to draw us into a set of assumptions and the way the debate is shaped by the use of language. We hope you, our readers, will join us to reconsider child protection and safeguarding children from abuse and neglect.

Child protection in this collection refers to state intervention in the lives of families by professionals; in most cases this is underpinned by child welfare statutes. Systems of child protection are not the result of accident, 'a force majeure', they are the consequence of human agency. They are more than the visible structures and depend on the grand edifices of state oversight, local arrangements and individual patterns of human relations. The first two are outwardly visible; the third is underlying, latent and often inaudible in public accounts. In every instance, systems of child protection produce something both the same and different each time. It is important not to conflate any of these systems with individual practitioners. The provisions of any system set a background for practitioners' actions; yet their individual actions are not synonymous with the system.

We are interested in child protection from a practitioner's location working with families and their children, not in any one protocol or single policy or particular structure and without fear or favour to any one system of child protection. We recognise the difficulty of ever achieving 'unbiased comprehension' (Sen 2009, p.161) of child abuse and neglect and of systems of child protection. Our familiarity with current thinking can limit our capacity for 'open impartiality' (Sen 2009, p.162): what we see and understand is not independent of our positions as observers; not one of us can take 'the view from nowhere – it is always from a delineated somewhere' (p.160). Our editorial viewpoints are influenced by our backgrounds in social work education, child welfare research and professional practice primarily based within the UK. Part of our position is a concern with the significance of social marginalisation and the control of life in systems of child protection (Waterhouse and McGhee 2014).

The authors we approached did not spring out of the blue. They were invited to contribute because of their expertise in social work, social science and humanities research. We asked them to draw on their disciplinary perspectives to examine the social problem of child abuse and neglect and the human and societal response. The writing of each author is done from her or his individual position and the chapters are structured to provide a bridge into research literature. This book is organised in three parts. Each part identifies a significant challenge for safeguarding children: Part 1 addresses the treatment of children and is concerned with their social, legal and political position; Part 2 reviews research evidence spanning a range of methods and countries to identify salient findings; Part 3 considers a third challenge – working with families and their children, paying particular attention to practice.

In this introductory chapter we draw on a close reading of all our authors' chapters to consider questions from this range of challenges that have puzzled us for some time. Three questions stand out for us, namely: why are children harmed; what does the shifting language of child protection represent; and which narratives from research need greater attention?

Why are children harmed?

Violence is an integral part of human societies and yet as a human condition it is present in each of us as a capability, as is a capacity to reject violence. We are surrounded every day by violence as manifest in slow starvation and disease that destroys socially marginalised human beings. It defies easy categorisation and is moderated to distinguish between apparently acceptable and unacceptable expressions, what is deemed legitimate and illegitimate violence, what attracts sanctions, what is permissible, the visibility of the violence and whether the underlying aims are rational and strategic or gratuitous. Most violence is not seen as deviant but is seen to be fulfilling political or societal goals. Violence can never be understood wholly in physical terms alone and includes violations of personal dignity and human worth; violence has a human face (Scheper-Hughes and Bourgois 2004). At the same time it is part of the human condition to go on as normal, to hold misery at arm's length even when close to home (Scheper-Hughes and Bourgois 2004, p.26). Nader (1997, p.22, cited in Scheper-Hughes and Bourgois 2004) defines violence as 'encompassing all forms of "controlling processes" that assault basic freedoms and individual or collective survival'.

The global nature of violence towards children has been mapped in a United Nations Secretary-General's Study on Violence against Children (Pinheiro 2006). The study portrays a comprehensive picture of the reality of violence against children around the world. The report documents violence experienced, not only in the home and family, but also in schools and educational settings, in care and justice systems, in work settings and in communities. Graça Machel (1996) in her report to the United Nations vividly portrays how children have become targets and are not merely bystanders in the brutality of armed conflict.

In this book, Walter Lorenz (Chapter 1) provides an historical analysis of the treatment of children and the profoundly political nature of childhood as a public and individual concern. He sees children as 'the ultimate test case of our modern conception of citizenship in this conflicting force field' (p.30). He emphasises for all of us, as citizens, the importance of belonging to a 'social unit', of the significance of social bonds and of the dangers of isolation.

Heather Montgomery (Chapter 2) as a social anthropologist alerts us that harm to children arises in all human societies and reminds us that parents exert control over children from the moment they are born: 'they decide what they will eat, how their bodies will be cared for, what rituals they will undergo, who is allowed to hold them and care for them, what they should wear and how they will be socialised and disciplined' (p.34). Pinheiro's United Nations study (2006) explicitly acknowledges the need to address the fact that 'the belief that adults have unlimited rights in the upbringing of a child compromises any approach to stop and prevent violence committed within the home, school or state institution' (p.xviiii).

Montgomery makes the point that children's voices have been notably absent in debates about what constitutes harm, causing their own insights and experiences to become invisible. Anthropologists have begun to uncover their views and Montgomery discusses studies that render more visible the harm done to children within cultural practices and the importance of listening to children's perceptions of such practices as a necessary balance. Tarja Pösö (Chapter 7), drawing on self-report studies, brings to our attention that children are exposed to higher levels of violence than adults.

E. Kay M. Tisdall (Chapter 3), writing from a children's rights perspective, confronts the continuing violence experienced by many children across cultures and contexts. Tisdall suggests, not without critique, that a universal children's rights framework by giving status to children in their own right opens one way, conceptually and legally, to challenge and to outlaw all violence to children around the world.

Jason Hart (Chapter 4) offers a different proposition when conceptualising threat in settings of armed conflict and political violence – aside from injury and death, young people may experience multiple and interrelated serious violations including coerced recruitment to military groups, denial of food and medical care, forced displacement associated with early marriage and child labour to reduce burdens on household units. Forms of abuse and neglect conventionally addressed by social workers in non-conflict settings are also found creating what he calls an interrelated web of protection concerns. Hart links the personal and political when he suggests that children seeking to protect themselves from violations of everyday settings in home and community may engage with military groups to protect themselves from personal violence. He gives the example of a young female member of an armed group in Colombia: 'The day I got my uniform I understood that no one can harm me now' (p.52). He finds in ethnographic studies of specific conflict-affected locations evidence that young people's experience of injustice in everyday life can lead them to engage in various forms of combat. Here he confronts the conceptual challenge that for some young people the pursuit of dignity and human worth may take precedence over physical wellbeing.

Andrew Cooper (Chapter 12) comes at the question of harm to children from a relational position that admits an emotional and intellectual readiness to face extremely discomforting, disturbing emotional truths about what might be happening to children in families and care systems. Drawing on his extensive clinical and research experience, he is able to say that few of us (in our day-to-day professional lives) are really comfortable with the thought or the feeling we may be 'in the presence of violent, damaging, sexually aggressive or neglectful behaviour' (p.145) which may limit our capacity to recognise what may be happening

The first question of why children are harmed is important because of its very opacity and the possibility of losing sight of this question in formulating research to mitigate child abuse and neglect. We think this question opens up the possibility of a more finely grained analysis of the violence children experience in their everyday lives across the world and in multiple settings. Our authors leave us in no doubt of the need to consider the question of harm from the viewpoints of all actors and to be mindful in the creation of imagery and that no further harm is caused.

What does the shifting language of child protection represent?

In this collection we are trying to grapple with the complex, shifting language of child abuse and neglect and child protection, where the same words are used to mean different things at different times and different words may be used to mean the same things. In doing so we have observed a metamorphosis of language, encompassing vocabularies sometimes used interchangeably – cruelty to children, non-accidental injury, battered baby syndrome, at risk, child abuse and neglect, child maltreatment, child protection, safeguarding, wellbeing, violence and injury prevention. The language is confusing, especially the apparent elision between the entity itself, child abuse and neglect, and the systems of child protection created to respond. In this collection we have tried to bring other vocabularies for thinking about child abuse and neglect and child protection. Pösö in Chapter 7 sets out a distinctive conceptual puzzle – how to address research in child abuse and neglect in the Finnish context, where national research communities do not use this expression. Instead, different terms are used within different disciplines – health and nursing researchers use 'child maltreatment' and social researchers use 'children exposed to violence' or 'family and domestic violence'. As editors we found a similar puzzle in attempting to reach a common vocabulary with our authors and the inevitable variation you will find is part of the landscape.

Does the way the language of child protection is articulated matter? Yes. Few of us would claim to be language experts and yet even a cursory familiarity with social science writing suggests the power of language and its ability to shape situations and practice; in other words, to have material effects on how we think and how we act. Child abuse and neglect and child protection are both slippery concepts: the first (child abuse and neglect), because of no agreed definition or broad and all-encompassing definitions with maltreatment of children subsumed under the rubric of violence and injury prevention (World Health Organization 2002); the second (child protection), because which the test to determine intervention is a moving marker, a shifting threshold, which when crossed is a starting point for involvement with public systems. A space has opened up for the extension of categories of harm to children, which become public categories of child abuse and neglect with associated lists of risk factors.

Risk is a highly charged concept both politically and morally, and 'naming a risk amounts to an accusation' (Douglas 1966, p.xix). The language of child abuse and neglect carries an accusation and a requirement for an account from the individual. Butler (2005) contrasts Nietzsche's (1969) argument that moral accountability only follows an accusation with her alternative idea of the importance of giving an account of oneself based neither on fear nor punishment, in other words, a non-accusatory, non-coercive approach that conveys an ethics of equality between parties (Lorraine Waterhouse and Janice McGhee, Chapter 11).

Sontag in her essays on illness as metaphor and against interpretation (in Cott 2013, p.25) writes 'don't make one thing into something else'; call it what it is without denial of what it is. This does not mean an avoidance of trying to explain or understand harms to children; on the contrary, it is to say plainly what you mean. Harm is harm. Cooper (Chapter 12) cautions us to think abut the language we deploy in discussing child protection work with families and their children. The use of metaphors akin to war – 'front line', 'bombardment' – may appear to be simple turns of phrase, yet as he suggests, without reflection these forms of speech may come to inhabit us. Why does this matter? Cooper suggests child protection may feel as if it is a warzone, but it is not a war, and the ultimate aim is to support children and help parents raise their children.

Which narratives from research need greater attention?

We asked our authors to identify key research in their disciplines or localities that they considered deserved greater attention. Trevor Spratt (Chapter 6) observes that research into children's lives is now 'unbounded' by discipline, and signals the importance for social work (and we suggest all disciplines involved in safeguarding children) of appreciating and using research from neuroscience, psychology and medicine alongside social science and social work research. This unboundedness gives rise to multiple research narratives, each with their own motif, enriching our understanding beyond the limitations of any one research discipline. Reading the chapters has caused us to look at the problem of child abuse and neglect from first principles and to decipher propositions that may help to address this problem.

Do no harm

Tim Dare (Chapter 5) in discussing automated predictive risk modelling returns to first principles when he invokes the World Health Organization's Principle 2 that in order for screening to be ethical there should be a treatment for the condition or at least mitigation of risk – in essence a principle of doing no harm. He suggests that 'the availability of an effective intervention is a prerequisite to an ethical screening programme because the screening process or some set of responses to it may themselves be potentially harmful, and hence require the possibility of a countervailing benefit' (p.71). The programme of research commissioned by the Department of Health, *Child Protection: Messages from Research* (1995) found six out of seven children referred to child protection systems were neither placed on the child protection register nor offered any support. Dare reminds us that contact in itself, under the aegis of child protection, has the potential for good or harm for both child and parent. In a child protection context where parties have unequal resources and status this inherent exposure and vulnerability makes a primary ethical claim (Arendt 1958) for both practice and research.

Bad for children

Spratt (Chapter 6) substantiates what we all know about the treatment of children – child abuse and neglect is bad for them. For over half a century, research has been tracking the associations between adverse childhood experiences (including child abuse and neglect) and later outcomes in life including health. Child abuse and neglect is now recognised as a cause of some adult diseases – essentially late manifestations of the developmental problems of childhood. The point Spratt is making is we now think of child abuse and neglect as contrary to the rights of children and have a body of interdisciplinary evidence in line with this moral and legal position. In the same way as the connection between tobacco smoking and lung disease resulted in a cultural norm that smoking is bad for you and is linked to poor health, child abuse and neglect is coming to share a similar cultural status. This represents a more profound shift in thinking than may at first meet the eye, arguably requiring both collective and individual response.

Poverty counts

The significance of neglect in the spectrum of child maltreatment is receiving renewed interest. Neglect is not easily classified, covering children both in material need and those at risk of significant harm. Several of the authors in this book (Daniel – Chapter 10, Spratt – Chapter 6, Pösö – Chapter 7) show us the artificial border between need and risk in systems of child protection.

In Finnish research social inequalities are seen as relevant for neglect (poverty, exclusion from education and labour markets for example) but not for child abuse and violence (Pösö – Chapter 7). However, Pösö argues that even in child neglect the messages from research on social inequalities are not necessarily applied. Her explanation for this is that social inequalities research focuses on the macro level and child neglect research on the micro level of individual or family level problems. Hart (Chapter 4), referring to the institutional response to Iraqi refugees in Jordan, identifies a predominance of psychosocial programmes in a context where resettlement programmes were closing, opportunities for employment were inhibited and cash support was withdrawn. He enlarges on the wholly negative effect of these combined circumstances on the capacity of primary caregivers to protect the young.

Brigid Daniel (Chapter 10) discusses how to balance two competing narratives, where parents of children formally identified as neglected require empathic and supportive responses to the multiple hardships in their lives versus recognition of the highly damaging consequences of neglect for children in the short and long term. She argues that families need both protective support and supportive protection and, that systems of child protection need to be able to respond to both dimensions of the problem. Research by Hooper *et al.* (2007), as reported by Daniel, find parents believe professionals see neglect when the problem is really hardship, professionals, in contrast, are confident about the difference between the two. Spratt (reporting in this book on his studies of 2001 (Spratt 2001) and 2014 (Hayes and Spratt 2014)) finds that all referrals to the child welfare system (whether defined as in need or at risk) receive a 'child protection' response to varying degrees. We think the overriding message for research is the potential clash in perspectives between parents and professionals on the root causes of their difficulties and their solutions.

Connecting research

In a number of chapters (Arney, Bromfield and McDougall – Chapter 8, Pösö – Chapter 7, O'Donnell – Chapter 9) reference is made to expanding the scale of social work research in child protection. Traditionally, forms of research or analyses, at least in the UK, have concentrated on single case studies (including meta-analyses of serious case reviews, Brandon *et al.* 2012) and investigation through public inquiries including more recent inquiries into historic abuse (Shaw 2007); case series studies that draw on one or more local authorities within one jurisdiction, often without a comparator group (Farmer *et al.* 2011); cohort studies with a comparator group (Wade *et al.* 2010); and small-scale ethnographies or interview-based studies (Broadhurst *et al.* 2010; Forrester *et al.* 2008). Fiona Arney, Leah Bromfield and Stewart McDougall (Chapter 8) underscore the need for stocktaking in social work research.

Our authors introduce other avenues for research that depend on advancing technologies including using routinely collected administrative data across sectors and countries. Melissa O'Donnell (Chapter 9) outlines the rudiments of a public health approach informed by population-level research using de-identified administrative data to devise preventive strategies to protect children from harm. She further discusses the use of administrative data by Freisthler *et al.* (2007) for geographical mapping and spatial analysis to determine the prevalence of community-level child maltreatment. In this study the rate of entry to foster care was related to the number of bars in a local area. Pösö discusses national administrative and statistical registers in Finland that permit analysis of macro-level dynamics of social inequality, for example highlighting associations between long-term economic hardship and an increase in out-of-home placements (Hiilamo 2009).

For our own chapter (Chapter 11) we have chosen to concentrate on the position of women. The consequences, especially for women (and children) of new global problems including conflict and instability, inequality and organised crime are being accented (Ki-moon 2013). Women are increasingly the heads of households. There has been a doubling of the proportion of lone parents in six countries and regions (Sweden, England, New Zealand, Western Australia, Manitoba (Canada) and the US (OECD 2011; Wulczyn 2009)). Research on child abuse and neglect cannot be divorced from the position of women – *the* majority of social services clients are poor women (Marcenko, Lyons and Courtney 2011), and studies rarely disaggregate parents in their findings. A fuller grasp of the position of women in child protection benefits from drawing on research in the humanities, and in Chapter 11, we the editors, discuss Judith Butler's theory of recognition to analyse relations between parties of unequal status and resource.

We hope these chapters on challenging child protection and safeguarding children will act as a repository for all those concerned with the lives of children globally and the treatment of childhood.

PART 1

Challenge One: Examining Preconceptions About Childhood and Harm to Children

CHAPTER 1

The Treatment of Childhood

Walter Lorenz

Modern societies live off the legacy of the Enlightenment, which posited issues of personal freedom and integrity, safeguarded by universal rights, as central reference points for social order and integration. From this notion developed the concept of citizenship guaranteeing civil, political and social rights through which the relationship between individuals and the state became successively regulated (Marshall 1950). At the same time modernism was and still is driven by the desire for humans to gain mastery over phenomena that previously had been considered as 'fate' or as effects of 'nature' and therefore as inscrutable and haphazard.

The autonomy of the adult individual came to be the ideal of personal, social, economic and political aspirations. The realisation of this project did not, however, proceed in a linear fashion but was always fraught with tensions and indeed contradictions. These relate to the incompatibility of personal autonomy, which implies at least potentially the pluralisation of standpoints and of standards of behaviour, with the universality claimed by rationality and particularly purposeful rationality. According to Weber (1947), standards derived from the latter mark, the advance not just of science and technology in modernity, but also the advance of bureaucracy and its accompanying legal regulations, which impinge progressively on all aspects of life, down to the sphere of the private.

The resulting restrictions on personal liberty are legitimated with reference to the human capacity to argue and to act rationally and hence in accordance with the legal and bureaucratic limits. This implies that non-rational behaviour has no place in modern societies, at least not in the public sphere. Bringing societies to adhere to these standards, to strive for rational standards within which the mature individual can enjoy freedom, is described as the civilising process administered conjointly by the typically modern institutions of policing, of education and to some extent of welfare (Wagner 1994). Yet all those measures have their limits when it comes to respect for the private sphere, where individual standards, convictions, cultural traditions and lifestyles are considered as sacrosanct even when they are seen as irrational.

Children in modernity

In the context of this project, children and the treatment of childhood play a very significant role. On the one hand, a child's individual course of development from a state of '*Unmündigkeit*' (a key term in Kant's characterisation of what the project of the Enlightenment seeks to overcome, which can be variously translated as 'tutelage', 'minority', 'immaturity' or 'dependency') to maturity and autonomy requires an organised educational effort that imparts, imbues or imposes (according to the various pedagogical methods and principles) the 'right' standards of a mature society. On the other hand, the unhindered (and only 'guided') unfolding of innate individual abilities towards a state of autonomy in full recognition of differences of ability and taste can be seen, from the perspective of reform pedagogy from Pestalozzi to Freire (Oelkers 2005), as the precondition for the development of a free and in that sense truly modern society. And while the establishment of compulsory schooling transferred this dilemma to the level of a public debate over educational methods and national standards in schools, the private and informal dimension of education is still difficult to subsume under such general principles since the family occupies principally the private sphere and hence the realm of freedom and autonomy.

Therefore, in considering issues concerning the welfare of children both in terms of the standards this implies and the methods to ensure the wellbeing of children, two fundamental lines of argument, typical of modernity, collide: from an individualist point of view, the standards according to which children are to be brought up are a private affair where personal, but also religious and other ideological considerations are the responsibility of private families or of private institutions, while from a collectivist point of view, children are already members of society from birth and their upbringing is a matter of public concern. This has to relate to universal standards, standards determined either by the inherent nature of the child or legitimated by the universal standards of reason, which every rational being would apply in caring for children.

The precondition for this was, however, that childhood became a recognised concept and children became publicly visible in their own right (Maynard and Thomas 2009). Before this became possible through the combined political efforts for cultural and legal changes, modernity had first demonstrated its other fundamental ambiguity in relation to children. Rather than including them in the modern aspiration for liberation, children were exposed and subjected to the technical capacity of modernity for ever more pervasive and effective forms of oppression under the dictate of purposeful rationality (Horrell and Humphries 1995). Their exploitation and suffering in the early phases of the industrial revolution was for a long time justified with reference to 'economic necessity' and compounded by the absence of 'voice' with which at least the oppressed adult could mobilise resistance against their plight (Hindman 2009). Children depended on intermediaries who were a long time coming.

Children between private and public concerns

It is therefore understandable that the possibility of raising issues concerning the plight of children to the level of public attention and debate rested on two conditions: it required recognition for the personhood of children despite their greater dependency on others; and it required a public readiness to argue for legitimate access to the private sphere so that a full picture of what practices lay hidden behind the façade of the private could be obtained. It is furthermore understandable that those mandated to act upon these concerns in the interest of the public are bound to walk into controversy, both from persons representing the private sphere (i.e. the individual families or carers who resent any such interference) and in the eyes of the public itself, which demands adherence to common standards of 'humane behaviour' and freedom from state interference at the same time. Here the dilemma of care and control in social services is being acted out in all its irreconcilable contradictions (Hauss 2008).

When in recent decades in many countries the deficits, failures and violations of standards of child welfare in private contexts (of family and of care institutions) were exposed to raise consternation and demands for effective intervention, this signalled a new phase of modernisation and was to some extent the result of the radicalisation of the inherent contradictions of modernity. Globalisation as the phenomenon of the relativising of economic, national and cultural boundaries raises with renewed urgency the question of how universal standards can be squared with individual choices. Global and instant communication facilities create an immediacy that brings the plight of sufferers worldwide to the attention of a virtual community and trigger heightened demands for universal and equal standards of conditions and treatments. Violence in particular touches universal sensibilities, especially when it was hitherto sanctioned by cultural conventions or traditional customs and when it affects women and children. At the same time the value of individual lifestyle choices and the demand for the recognition of differences in the private sphere becomes equally more pronounced and leads to the opposite trend of greater tolerance towards cultural diversity, not least in the choice of types of partnerships and family models. The de-standardisation of family patterns in the wake of these developments has a major and frequently detrimental impact on children's welfare because of those contradictory developments (Lee 2001).

It is significant that in 2014 the United Nations Children's Fund produced a report that draws urgent attention to the extent of the suffering children are still exposed to in countries all over the world (United Nations Children's Fund 2014). It documents not just the continued existence of 'traditional' forms of violence against children and young people but also the extension of violence into the new private realms, for instance of the internet, as well as the recognition of previously trivialised forms of violence such as sexual violence, bullying and corporal punishment. At the same time, the report evidences wide discrepancies in the extent to which such forms of violence are being uniformly recognised or condemned, which explains greatly varying rates of reporting.

Beyond childrens' right

Where a few decades ago the international effort was concentrated on defining universal standards and enshrining them in the form of the *Convention on the Rights of the Child* (United Nations 1989), this latest report is a damning indictment of the ineffectiveness of mere declarations and gives renewed impetus to the critique that this ineffectiveness is directly connected to the presumed universality of the Convention (see Tisdall, Chapter 3, p.43) in addition to profound criticism of the Convention reflecting a typically Western conception of the child (Kaime 2011). Furthermore, while adults and particularly action groups representing the civil rights of adults have been able to make better use of human rights declarations, children themselves cannot form a lobby and cannot therefore gain unmediated access to the core achievements of modernity. They remain largely dependent on advocacy by professionals, activists and politicians and their situation is therefore particularly complex: 'The universality of childhood and the diversity of children's real lives are difficult to reconcile' (Stoecklin and Bonvin 2014, p.8).

The discourse on the universal and equal rights of children appeared to put a definitive line between culturally embedded practices of pre-modern times (see Montgomery, Chapter 2), such as abandoning unwanted or burdensome children in the wilderness, practising paedophilia, chastising children violently or treating them as objects of economic exploitation, and a modern conception of childhood as a protected space, a moratorium in which children enjoyed equal recognition of their freedom to grow. But it became equally apparent that cultural differences could not be eliminated or ignored under conditions of modernity as the emphasis on religious freedom for instance shields practices like circumcision of boys or genital mutilation of girls from legal sanctions in some jurisdictions. Even the debate on abortion and the rights of the unborn child can be seen as part of this controversy and demonstrates the limits that references to universal rationality or to normativity derived from medical evidence pose on effective interventions (Cornock and Montgomery 2011).

The contrast between universality and relativity in relation to childhood is compounded by the difference between a psychological and a sociological perspective. The reference to psychological 'constants' in terms of culture-independent needs of children at the various stages of psychological development has helped underpin efforts in applying human rights to children. Two developments came together in this regard.

Recognising child abuse

On the medical side new and convincing evidence was collected on the nature of particular child injuries observed by medical staff in emergency situations. This led to the identification and diagnostic application of what was provocatively termed the 'battered child syndrome' (Kempe *et al.* 1962) after previous references to 'non-accidental injuries' had received little public attention (Krugman and Korbin 2013). The framing of such incidents as a 'syndrome' triggered a painful process of gradual realisation that the advent of 'modern, civilised societies' had not spelled the end of inhumane childrearing practices. And under conditions of modernity it was not sufficient to attribute this to 'moral failings' on the part of the perpetrators; their behaviour called for scientific explanations.

Therefore the systematic medical study and classification of child abuse and neglect was paralleled on the child psychology side by the pioneering work on early attachment around John Bowlby (1977, 1985), which evidenced the long-term effects of bond disruption, both for infant and caregivers. Looking back on the research of the Henry Kempe Centre, Ryan writes:

> In discovering the ability to foresee the risk of serious physical abuse within the first hours and days of an infant's interaction with the caregiver, the protective properties of secure attachment became evident. In time, the understanding that abuse is, at its core, a disorder of attachment emerged. (Ryan 2013, p.17)

These research findings placed the damaging effects of physical, emotional and sexual maltreatment of children inescapably not just in the professional but also in the public domain. On the basis of the pressure for changes in practices generated by them, they gradually found entry not just into professional childcare and protection practices in many countries with advanced social welfare systems, but they were also taken up by legislation and the practice of family law courts. The concern for the continuity of care in particular, most vociferously expressed by a Freudian group of psychoanalysts with their seminal book *Beyond the Best Interest of the Child* (Goldstein, Freud and Solnit 1973), led to faster decisions when placing children in care, or in divorce procedures.

Decision-makers relied on the availability of 'hard evidence' concerning the risks associated with children remaining in precarious care arrangements and interpreted 'the best interest of the child' in terms of the permanency of secure (alternative or still existing natural) bonds.

Equipped with such 'positive findings' and the corresponding diagnostic tools in the form of lists of indicators, social services in many countries embarked on a systematic review of family cases in collaboration with schools and medical services in order to obtain a full picture of 'children at risk'.

Risk reduction and modern insecurity

But precisely these developments brought the contradictory nature of modernity's rational-purposeful approach to problem solving to the surface in as much as the positivist paradigm on which it is based inevitably brought with it a concentration of power on expert systems at the expense of personal (and indeed also professional) liberty. The legal backing of child protection interventions, which gave professionals the power to investigate private family matters more effectively, paradoxically led to a weakening of the position of professionals who were once used to exercising professional discretion on the basis of their expert knowledge and who were now increasingly constrained to follow procedures in order to keep their decisions within legal parameters.

In the light of cases of suspected abuse not being followed up, several countries introduced 'at risk registers' with the result that for instance in Australia up to one in five children will be the subject of a child protection notification before they reach the age of 15 (see Arney, Bromfield and McDougall, Chapter 8). In many ways the emphasis thereby changes from child protection or child welfare to risk management, not least when professionals themselves come under pressure to justify their actions (of either not having intervened sufficiently promptly or of having acted prematurely and with insufficient respect for families' rights to privacy).

Undoubtedly there has been a lack of systematic statistical analyses of risk factors associated with child maltreatment (see O'Donnell in this volume, p.114). Large-scale statistical databases, such as those now being established for instance in New Zealand (see Dare, Chapter 5) can claim to capture a greater number of children at risk and at earlier crisis points, but as in other areas of public order where improved surveillance can lead to better levels of public security, the ethical contentious issues arising from such measures are considerable (Munro 2007).

The paradox observed in other sociological contexts where the advent of 'risk society' has meant an ever increasing sense of uncertainty in the light of hazards being recast as 'avoidable risks' (Giddens 1991), extends, therefore, particularly to the area of social work with 'children at risk'. The trend towards the 'risk management of everything' is recognised by child welfare professionals as being detrimental to more effective ways of ensuring child welfare and is associated with a shift in professional orientation from prevention and crisis intervention to risk management (Power 2004).

The narrow targeting of risk factors and of families with a concentration of 'risk indicators' inevitably has a discriminatory effect that can only be partially counteracted by giving those family units priority access to welfare resources. Availing of welfare support services can in itself be stigmatising, particularly under the conditions of neoliberal ideology that have prevailed almost universally in social policies since the 1990s with their emphasis on self-sufficiency and the individual duty to self-support in crises. This has resulted in a general framing of child abuse research as an individualistic search for causes at the expense of a wider socio-political perspective (Schmid 2015).

Child protection or child welfare

These developments are associated with a redistribution of public resources for child protection instead of child welfare or indeed family welfare. A risk perspective can easily lead to a polarisation between attention support and protection, with protection gaining priority because its effects – and hence the 'efficiency' of the allocation of resources – can be measured more easily. Commenting on developments in the UK, Spratt (Chapter 6) notices a shift in academic and practice attention towards a protection agenda, with the paradoxical effect that 'children have to be designated as in need of protection to access services and, as a consequence, services to the wider population of "Children in Need" remain underdeveloped' (p.84).

The effects of a preoccupation with risk reduction extend equally to children and to the professionals themselves who come under pressure to 'cover themselves' against accusations of ineffective and inappropriate interventions. Furthermore, reports indicate that an increase in competences concerning the identification of symptoms of violence and abuse do not necessarily translate into corresponding competences in treating the results and in changing abusive behaviour (e.g. Øverlien 2010).

To counteract these deleterious effects, Finnish child and family social policies for instance deliberately moved away from the concept of 'abuse and neglect', and with the Act of 1983 instead emphasised again support services to families and children in need (see Pösö, Chapter 7). But as Parton (2011) observes with regard to social and political developments in the UK, it is not enough for government policies to replace the reference to protection with one to welfare when access to welfare resources is still premised on the risk indicators of particular families.

Furthermore, this raises the issue of how welfare support is to reach children since assistance reaches them only through families or family-like settings. And as these diversify, the 'unit of care' becomes again a contested reference point: 'Because the family had been both deconstructed and disaggregated, children and parents (both men and women) were seen to inhabit much more separate worlds with somewhat separate interests' (Parton 2011, p.857). Parton goes on to comment on the private/public split: 'while "partnering" was seen as essentially a private matter, subject to individual freedom of action and choice, "parenting" was very much a public concern and therefore a legitimate site for state intervention' (Parton 2011, p.857).

These dilemmas indicate that safeguarding the welfare of children in this phase of modernity involves addressing some of the fundamental dichotomies that characterise the project of modernity, such as that between personal freedom and universal equality and equal rights, and this means principally to treat them dialectically rather than furthering their polarisation. It can already be observed that in many countries private welfare organisations are being delegated to provide programmes and measures of prevention while acute crisis intervention is concentrated in public hands, and this accentuates the splitting between 'care and control' that social work as a profession had always sought to keep together and thereby to transform the polarity.

In order to move beyond polarisation a reference to the political construction of childhood becomes inevitable. The different perspectives assembled in this volume show convincingly that wherever childhood or the needs of the child are being defined from one framework alone, be that a reference to biology, psychology, culture or rights, there is a danger of turning children into objects, even where this means objects of well-meaning intentions. 'Deficits' noted in the social sphere are never merely objective factors but are always associated with social values and hence raise the suspicion of being the result of individual 'failings', unless the political conditions are created for the elimination or prevention of the resulting discrimination.

Equally, giving way to the popular intellectual stance of 'post-modern indifference' in the light of the individualisation and relativisation of positions and approaches to childhood would simply be irresponsible in relation to the tangible concerns and needs of children. The fact that politics have a central role to play – not just in raising public awareness, creating legal instruments for protection and ensuring substantial child welfare measures, but also in terms of the impact of different political cultures on practice – is reflected in the different degrees to which social workers and social services are being scapegoated for failures to protect children from harm.

Treating children within different 'welfare regimes'

It is significant that in Europe the most ardent criticism of that profession's failings in cases of child abuse with lethal outcome was levelled at social workers in the UK, a country with a pronounced liberal political culture where the line between private and public concerns is stringently drawn (and yet hotly contested when it comes to 'control in the public interest').

Responses in Nordic countries have largely existed in a scientific search for structural explanations, as demonstrated in Chapter 7 on Finland by Pösö. Here the state is (still) expected to be the principal provider of welfare, with all the paternalist implications and restrictions on personal freedom that might entail but which that political culture is prepared to bear. In countries with an emphasis on the subsidiarity principle in welfare, such as Germany or Austria, the relationship between the private and the public sphere is mediated by numerous non-governmental service providers whose mandate is to be closer to the culturally defined interests of service users in the diversity of civil society interests they represent. This diffuses the critique on a single profession or institution in cases of failure, which of course occur in all 'regimes', but also slows down a concerted response to the issue.

This typology is not meant to idealise one political tradition over others – indeed there are merits and demerits to be found in each one. But it is meant to underline the necessity of considering the central contribution of politics as a platform on which different interests can be brought together and priorities be argued out from different positions. Modern democracies have played a central role in constituting the personhood of citizens, reluctantly in many instances as was the case with regard to women, but nevertheless in an inexorable drive towards recognising, establishing and safeguarding the rights of human beings to their fundamental dignity and to create a political community based on principles of equality. The very concept of citizenship testifies to this unfinished process of recognition; unfinished particularly in the sense that the conditions under which citizenship is being afforded are still contested between an unconditional right to belong for all who have 'connections' (by birth, residence or 'blood') to the political territory of a nation state and an emphasis on conditions under which a person has to 'earn' citizenship (language, behaviour adjustment, payment etc.).

Children are the ultimate test case of our modern conception of citizenship in this conflicting force field. However, it is clear on the one hand that on account of their dependency on others their rights to belong not just to their biological carers but also to a political community from birth (or earlier) need to be promoted all the more; on the other hand, this must not imply that their needs can be standardised and that the care they require must be provided predominantly from the public side. Where this basic political structure is absent, as is the case in war situations or in anarchic post-conflict situations, children are all the more drawn into the ugliest form of political activity, the resort to open violence. Under these conditions, as Hart documents and analyses (Chapter 4), children as street gangs (Aptekar and Stoecklin 2014) and as child soldiers take to violence not necessarily by force or to protect themselves, but to claim the recognition that no formal institution is able to provide them in those circumstances.

Children and the capability approach

In terms of the recognition of the necessary interweaving of rights, resources and non-material support, the attempts of promoting a 'capability approach' particularly in relation to children appears to be very promising on account of its comprehensive orientation (Stoecklin and Bonvin 2014). The capability perspective, proposed by Sen (2005) and Nussbaum (2011) examines the conditions for freedom on the basis of the interplay between resources and individual abilities and emphasises the 'necessary presence of individual and social parameters that act as facilitators for the conversion of resources or commodities into capabilities' (Bonvin and Stoecklin 2014, p.3).

In relation to children this can mean a regard for 'evolving capabilities' (Biggeri, Ballet and Comim 2011) in recognition of the dialectic developmental interplay between dependence on the provision of help and resources from others and the assertion of individual agency and hence freedom by the child's 'self' (Dixon and Nussbaum 2012). Bearing this dual orientation in mind can give professionals operating in the area of child welfare and child protection a basis for resisting attempts at forcing a split orientation in their actions and for safeguarding the integrity and rights of children without denying them their agency. This is the core of competence in childcare.

Overcoming this split poses more generally the fundamental challenge of our current era and of our confrontation with the effects of modernity. It invariably requires getting involved in normative questions, which cannot be reduced to technical or scientific issues in the positivist sense but involve political issues like poverty and inequality (Featherstone, White and Morris 2014). Such normative issues require constant negotiation, which means explicit references to political processes in as much as norms are never just given but become norms through participative negotiation.

Working with children – political dimensions

Concretely, this implies that social work in the area of child welfare in particular can only be effective if it operates on two levels simultaneously. These include, first, direct personal work in situations of crisis. This requires scientific knowledge of how to recognise and interpret failures and deficits according to objective criteria and correspondingly the competences in finding effective solutions to prevent further harm and opening pathways for children to those conditions that meet their developmental needs; and second, political negotiation promoting a shared understanding for the required resources and opportunities is needed. In addition, and above all, the inevitable unpredictability of human agency (see Waterhouse and McGhee, p.9; Cooper p.142) has to be taken into account, which forms the basis both for considerations of prevention and for a critical sharing of responsibility in cases of 'failure'.

The political dimension of social work is not confined to lobbying and advocacy in the context of policy meetings and structures. Competences in enabling political change processes are also a feature of direct work at the personal level, where the tension between personal freedom and universal rights and obligations is most acute. If social work is to be more than therapy, counselling or indeed policing and to uphold the meaning of 'the social', it requires always a concern for making people belong to a social unit, not just in the psychological sense but also in a contractual sense as citizens.

Children per se as well as adults who 'fail in their duties', for whatever reason, are always in danger of not having their citizenship fully recognised or losing their citizenship status altogether, thereby being made the 'object' of decisions made by 'the system'. Children are citizens from birth. Without granting such basic political security, given by society 'in advance', no obligations can later be redeemed from them as adults. Without this precondition, no pedagogy aimed at fostering a commitment to common concerns that constitute a political community makes any sense.

Establishing and ensuring this 'reconnection' therefore also paves the way for professionals having the right to make legitimate demands on these citizens, old and young, including demands of legal compulsion. Practitioners know that the 'victim-perpetrator grid' is far too schematic and abstract to capture the actual complexity of situations of neglect and that the bifurcation between 'family support' and 'child protection' that is so prominent, for instance in the UK (see Chapter 10) but increasingly also in other countries, renders both measures less effective.

The relevance of social pedagogy

Methodologically, this perspective suggests the overdue dialogue between the paradigms of social work and of pedagogy, which has been almost totally neglected in the literature on approaches to child welfare (except the attempts by Petrie (2013) and Cameron (2013)). While the social pedagogy tradition per se is also affected by a deep division between instrumentalist approaches concentrating on behaviour change at the individual level and a holistic view that at times idealises a political change agenda, its central message is that coping with life's challenges is a general learning process that cannot be left to the responsibility of individuals but requires a collective effort and exchange on values, goals and the means of achieving them.

Competences in both 'protective support' and 'supportive protection' (see Daniel, Chapter 10) and their dialectical relationship have long been explored in the tradition of social pedagogy, not exclusively in relation to crisis situations where the welfare of children is at risk, but as a feature of 'social life' in general. Modernity has ultimately exposed individuals to the dangers of isolation and being left to their own devices, and it is not only children who suffer from the negation and disruption of social ties.

A comprehensive, non-punitive but effective approach to child welfare helps to re-establish those principles and values in societies that risk overloading individuals with responsibilities that they are incapable of shouldering alone. Overcoming 'tutelage' in Kant's sense in all its manifestations, while creating positive social bonds, remains the central challenge of our times; and heightened sensibilities with regard to the plight of children should constitute a shared commitment to this task.

CHAPTER 2

The Dynamics of Culture

Heather Montgomery

Parents exert control over children from the moment they are born: they decide what they will eat, how their bodies will be cared for, what rituals they will undergo, who is allowed to hold them and care for them, what they should wear and how they will be socialised and disciplined. One point of consensus among anthropologists is that each of these activities is culturally determined and while children are considered to have basic, unchanging, biological needs (for food, warmth etc.), how these needs are met depends on cultural context so that there is nothing natural or universal about the care and protection of children.

Whilst the overwhelming majority of parents throughout the world love and care for their children, there are widely different views about how best to treat them and how their needs and role in society should be understood. Despite recent rhetoric about equality and rights (*Convention on the Rights of the Child* – United Nations 1989), there are inherent power differentials between adults and children, and it is these differentials that present the possibility of abuse of the weak by the powerful, even in the most intimate of relationships.

Harm to children

Harm to children arises in all human societies and all human actors have the capacity to inflict harm on others and to resist so doing. Yet harm is a slippery concept and there is often limited consensus about how it is defined and how it can be recognised. Questions of what constitutes harm remain subjective, highly contested and emotive.

Looking cross-culturally, these issues are heightened and behaviour that seems self-evidently harmful to outsiders may seem very different from an emic (insider) perspective. Furthermore, definitions of harm differ within cultures as well as across them and, most importantly of all, will vary in relation to the role of the actors: a child who feels harmed will have a very different perspective to the person inflicting that harm. It is important to emphasise, therefore, that anthropologists cannot provide definitive answers about what practices and behaviours are harmful to children but can contribute to the debate by analysing conceptions of harm and providing an explanation of the context in which harm occurs.

One ethnographic example that shows up some of the many complexities of understanding harm to children is the pioneering work done by Nancy Scheper-Hughes (1992) in the shanty towns or *favelas* of north-east Brazil, where severe poverty is endemic and infant mortality rates very high. Scheper-Hughes details, with much sympathy, the neglect of young children who seem passive or sickly and the sometimes fatal harm done to infants by their mothers, who withhold food and offer low levels of emotional, physical and emotional support to those children whom they do not 'trust' to survive.

Mothers do not give these children medicine if they need it (and usually cannot afford to) and treat their deaths with indifference and resignation, using the same name for successive children and rarely mourning dead infants. More consciously, some mothers make the decision to withhold food from one child in order to give it to a more active or healthier child, or an older one, who is more likely to survive. Yet while Scheper-Hughes analyses the individual and social reactions of mothers to their children's death, she also emphasises the point that the harm to these children is not socially sanctioned or due to individual pathology but bound up with historical legacies of colonialism, the slave and sugar trades, endemic poverty and social disenfranchisement for these impoverished mothers.

Her work has been very influential both inside and outside anthropology but it has not gone unchallenged. The idea that in some cases mothers make conscious or unconscious choices about which children to neglect has been disputed. Nations and Rebhun (1988), for example, working in similar *favelas* to Scheper-Hughes, claim that they found no evidence of such neglect or harm among mothers, who strove against all odds to keep their children alive, taking them to traditional healers when bureaucratic and geographical constraints prevented them from accessing modern medical care.

They accepted that women did not and could not always breastfeed their children, did not always arrange prompt medical care and that, for some women, 'a sort of "twelve month pregnancy" may exist in which newborns are regarded more like fetuses than like children' (Nations and Rebhun 1988, p.190). However, they deny that this implies infant neglect or intentional harm. They claim that women are deeply attached to infants and that their lack of emotion in the face of their deaths has more to do with socially appropriate stoicism and Catholic beliefs about infants being transformed into angels than to any form of indifference, neglect or harm.

Another ethnographic example concerning the treatment of infants shows similar problems facing anthropologists when confronted with behaviour that apparently causes harm to children yet continues to be practised. Alma Gottlieb has worked extensively with a small group of subsistence farmers living on the edge of the rainforest in the Côte d'Ivoire – the Beng – and has focused on their children, analysing ideas about childhood and how children are socialised. She has described the high value placed on children and the love lavished on them as well as the elaborate series of rituals performed on newborn babies, such as painting their faces and bodies, piercing their ears or making them wear certain jewellery (Gottlieb 2004).

However, alongside these benign-sounding forms of infant care, the Beng also force-feed babies water before they are allowed to breastfeed and give them twice daily enemas from the day the umbilical stump falls off until they are around a year old (Gottlieb 2014). Gottlieb writes in detail about the symbolic meanings behind these two practices and why Beng mothers see them as positive for their children. She argues that in training the infant body in this way, mothers are asserting their rights to decide what goes into their children's bodies and over how these bodies should be socialised.

The mothers to whom Gottlieb talked emphasised that they saw these practices as beneficial to their children and they continued to administer enemas to them throughout their lives as well as giving them to other adults and administering them themselves. Training a child's bowels very early also has practical value in that mothers are forced to rely on babysitters to look after their children while they work and a baby who defecates randomly (rather than after an enema given in the morning and afternoon) will be difficult to look after and the mother may struggle to find a babysitter. This, Gottlieb argues, can have serious implications for the mother, her other children and for the wider community.

Gottlieb's discussion is highly nuanced, however, and she acknowledges that these practices are 'ultimately meant to be nurturing' but appear to use 'violent means' (2014, p.180). While she explains and understands why Beng mothers behave in this way, and argues that in the long term it might not cause lasting harm, she admits that it can be risky and is potentially harmful, given the possibility of infection through dirty water and the high levels of infant mortality in the region.

She also acknowledges that other anthropologists have not been so tolerant, quoting David Lancy, who describes the practice as 'deplorable' (Goftleib 2014, p.161). She concludes however:

> When infants are socialised into body-violating practices that are viewed not as punishment for rude or sinful behavior (as violence towards children is often justified by parents), but rather as beneficial both to themselves and to their mothers, the outside observer must pause to consider the possibility that long-term emotional damage is far from inevitable. (2014, p.177)

Cultural relativism and harm

Anthropologists have always argued that the moral frameworks of different cultures vary radically and need to be judged in their own terms. They have a long (and proud) tradition of defending non-Western cultures against accusations of ignorance, primitiveness, savagery, superstition and lack of sophistication, examining the internal logic, coherence and morality of the cultures they have studied. They have also argued that it is not the job of the anthropologist to intervene or attempt to make changes in the belief systems or behaviours of other people, and that their role is simply to observe, participate and analyse these worldviews (Montgomery 2013).

This is, of course, a somewhat unrealistic ideal, and is rarely put into practice even by those who articulated it most clearly (compare for example Malinowski's diaries (1967) with his published discussion (1922) of the fieldwork methods and the role of the anthropologist). Anthropologists have rarely been able to remain neutral, observe without intervening or leave their own morality aside. In terms of studying children, issues of neutrality and non-intervention become even more acute as anthropologists dissect the power relationships between adults and children and the structural inequalities between the local and the global that leave children vulnerable to harm. Against a backdrop of universal children's rights, and an imperative to carry out research in the best interest of the child and to the highest ethical standards, few anthropologists have found it easy or desirable to maintain the role of the detached relativist who analyses without judging.

An excellent example of these difficulties can be found in the work of Helen Kavapalu, who has carried out extensive fieldwork on childrearing in Tonga, focusing particularly on discipline (1993). She describes a society in which children are regularly beaten by adults and other children. Punishments can be severe and children are beaten from a young age. Children are expected to endure punishment without crying and to apologise in a quiet, monotonous voice; and those beating the child, or witnessing the beating, often laugh when doing so. Physical punishment is thought to teach children emotional and behavioural self-control and to ensure that they conform to social ideals of respect and obedience. It is also explicitly talked about as a way of teaching a child about social hierarchies and a way of enforcing the power relationships between adults and children. It is even seen, by some, in terms of concern and love, and Kavapalu quotes one informant who claims, 'Parents are said to punish their children "because of their love"' (1993, p.319).

Although these beatings can be painful and humiliating for a child, they are not random acts of violence but linked to wider ideas about the nature of childhood and how children should be socialised. While appearing harsh to outsiders, they are not necessarily seen as ill-intentioned or morally wrong within their own context. Despite her careful analysis of this, however, Kavapalu remained morally conflicted over what she witnessed in Tonga and was unconvinced that such punishments did no harm. Even while understanding why parents beat their children, she found it hard not to judge. She recognised her own ambivalence as well as that of the children and adults she worked with: 'Since punishment is positively valued as a form of teaching and an expression of love and concern, the distinction between protecting/providing and hurting is somewhat blurred, and the ambivalence that results is deep-seated and complex' (Kavapalu 1993, p.321).

Kavapalu also contrasts her own responses with those of previous anthropologists who looked at child discipline in Tonga and, in doing so, she shows how ideas about the value of cultural relativism within anthropology are highly problematic. She quotes the discrepancies apparent in earlier studies of Tonga carried out by Pearl and Ernest

Beaglehole, who, in their field notes, spoke of the sadism of the beatings carried out by parents and the agony of the children. In their diaries they give an account of a mother 'beating her child with thwarted fury that seems nine parts pure sadism and one-quarter part altruistic-disciplinary. To us, as we watch the scene, these child beatings seem to exceed all that is reasonable and just' (quoted in Kavapalu 1993, p.313). In the Beagleholes' published work, however, this shock at the severity of the beatings and their view that this was abusive are transformed into the bland statement: 'The child who disobeys or who is thought to be lazy in carrying out a command is generally severely beaten by the mother. The beatings [...] appear to be village-practice in enforcing discipline' (quoted in Kavapalu 1993, p.313). While this latter statement may conform more closely to anthropological ideals of dispassionate observation, it clearly negates and suppresses the very real harm done to the children by disciplining them in this way; harm that Kavapalu understands and explains but does not condone, justify, or perhaps most importantly of all, render invisible.

What constitutes harm will always be contested, but the work of anthropologists focusing directly on childhood has highlighted the dangers that children are exposed to and the possibility of harm that is inherent not only in the family but also in the wider environment. Significantly, they have also shown that talking to children themselves reveals very different ideas about what constitutes harm and it is children's voices that have been so noticeably lacking in this debate.

To give another brief example, patterns of child fostering have been well studied by anthropologists in West Africa for over 50 years, particularly those of the Gonja, the Yoruba or the Mende (Goody 1982). This work has looked at why children were sent away, often for large parts of their childhood, to live with distant relatives in different parts of the country. Various explanations have been given, ranging from giving children to childless couples to raise, to providing domestic labour for others, to giving children a means of social mobility by placing them in the houses of more powerful kin. Interviews with adults suggest that these placements are usually seen positively and some parents argue that 'the truly unfortunate children are those who have not been sent away from home to advance' (Bledsoe 1990, p.85). Yet when anthropologists talked directly to children, they found very different responses and many children described being fostered as a miserable experience that brought them into conflict with both their birth parents and their foster parents.

One study of fostered children in Cameroon showed that they were highly ambivalent about their experience and described being fostered as a time of conflict and tension (Notermans 2008). Bledsoe (1990) also cites examples of children being treated harshly by their foster parents and of their biological parents being generally unsympathetic to their complaints, an attitude that the children interpreted as a form of neglect and even abuse.

Gaining a children's perspective underlines the point that culture is not monolithic and different actors have very different relationships to experiences of harm. Furthermore, such work acknowledges that some practices, however longstanding and however much a part of cultural history and identity, do damage children, and that 'culture' is no protection against harm: what has long been considered socialisation and discipline can be seen very differently if looked at through the lens of child welfare and wellbeing. This is not to suggest that there is no room for cultural variation in raising children or that all harm towards children could be eliminated if only all parents worked to the same model and raised their children in the same way. It does suggest, however, that culture is not neutral, that certain cultural practices may benefit some and harm others and that, as anthropologist and children's rights activist Judith Ennew has argued so cogently, '[w]hile cultural context must be respected, it is important to note that culture is not a "trump card" in international human rights' (1998, p.8).

Furthermore, just as culture is not monolithic, nor is it static. Culture is endlessly dynamic and changing and 'traditional' practices can and do change in response to internal and external forces. In the case of Tonga, Kavapalu (writing later as Morton) found that the introduction of the United Nations *Convention on the Rights of the Child* (1989), changes in government legislation, and newer ideas about parent/child relationships, meant that attitudes towards child punishment had changed significantly since her initial fieldwork. She found there had been a re-evaluation of traditional ideas about punishment and the harm it may or may not do to children and while physical punishment had not disappeared, there was much less reliance on it and it was less harsh than she had previously witnessed (Morton 1996).

In West Africa, too, fostering is being critically re-examined by both parents and children. In Nigeria, Renne (2005) describes how there is now a greater unease about sending children away to be fostered. Parents speak of their concerns and worries, while children are running away from what they perceive as abusive foster carers. Many of the younger generation of parents feel that they are the best people to raise children and are limiting their family sizes so that they have only those children they can care for themselves.

Conclusion

This anthropologically informed comment on harm to children has shown children's vulnerability and the widespread risks that children face wherever they are in the world. The power differentials between adults and children exist even in the most loving and intimate relationships, and the possibility of harm exists both within the family and the wider society. Children, however, have rarely been asked for their own perceptions of harm, causing their own experiences and insights to become invisible.

Anthropologists have started to uncover these views, examining how structures and practices that have long been considered necessary, and even beneficial, to children, might now be considered harmful. Appeals to respect and uphold cultural difference, while important, are not always adequate when it comes to preventing harm to children; and adults and children may have very different perceptions about the necessity and benefits of continuing with some traditions.

It is imperative, therefore, that both adults' and children's views are taken into account in any discussions of harm, thereby making harm to children more visible and more likely to be challenged.

CHAPTER 3

The Rule of Law

E. Kay M. Tisdall

Introduction

Children's rights has become an increasingly prevalent and persuasive framework for child protection in the UK and internationally. The international and regional human rights regimes have always included children within their remits, along with adults. The particular expression and consolidation of these, for children, was provided by the United Nations (UN) *Convention on the Rights of the Child* (UNCRC) in 1989. Since then it has become the most ratified human rights treaty, with only the United States of America not yet having done so. The UNCRC has inspired certain changes in how children are conceptualised. Rather than passive and vulnerable dependants, children are recognised as social actors in their families and communities; rather than the property of their parents and objects of state intervention, children have status in their own right, are the subjects, service users and sometimes clients of state intervention and services – including child protection services.

Such changing ideas of children parallel certain changes in the protection of children from harm over the centuries – where the state has been recognised as having a role to intervene in the private life of families – and challenge current ones – like the continuing violence experienced by many children, across cultures and contexts. Concerns about the extent of this violence led the UN to fund a worldwide study (United Nations Secretary-General 2006), the UN Committee on the Rights of the Child to organise *General Comment No. 13* (published 2011) to address it and subsequently the UN to appoint a Special Representative of the Secretary-General on Violence against Children.

Bessell and Gal (2009) propose that human rights can be understood at two levels: 'first, as the international system of treaties, visionary statements and commitments, and second as a conceptual framework that shapes action' (p.286). This chapter begins by setting out key elements of the international legal system in relation to children's rights and violence against children, focusing on the UNCRC and the UN Committee's *General Comment No. 13*. The chapter then concentrates on the rights framework conceptually: what the concept of rights offers, and a leading alternative expressed by legal theorists, 'vulnerability'. The chapter concludes by (re)considering children's rights' contribution to the protection of children, with both the advantages and disadvantages of this legal and conceptual framework.

The UN Convention on the Rights of the Child

The UNCRC broadly addresses children under the age of 18 (unless majority is attained earlier, Article 1) and covers a wide range of issues, from justice to health, within its 54 Articles. While the UNCRC should be considered holistically (UNCRC 2003), there are four key principles: non-discrimination (Article 2); a child's best interests are a primary consideration in all actions concerning children (Article 3); a child's rights to survival and development (Article 6); and a child's right to express views freely in all matters affecting the child (Article 12).[1] According to the UNCRC and international law, ratification of the Convention means that States Parties are obligated to implement the UNCRC (see Article 4). To aid interpretation and promote implementation, the UN Committee issues General Comments. Of particular note for this chapter is the *General Comment No. 13: The Right of the Child to Freedom from All Forms of Violence* (United Nations Committee on the Rights of the Child 2011). This General Comment echoes the World Report (United Nations Secretary-General 2006), in stating 'no violence against children is justifiable; all violence against children is preventable' (United Nations Committee on the Rights of the Child 2011, p.3).

Article 19 is the key article for the General Comment. As written in the UNCRC, Article 19 states:

---

1   See: www.ohchr.org/en/professionalinterest/pages/crc.aspx.

1. States Parties shall take all appropriate legislative, administrative, social and educational measures to protect the child from all forms of physical or mental violence, injury or abuse, neglect or negligent treatment, maltreatment or exploitation, including sexual abuse, while in the care of parent(s), legal guardian(s) or any other person who has the care of the child.

2. Such protective measures should, as appropriate, include effective procedures for the establishment of social programmes to provide necessary support for the child and for those who have the care of the child, as well as for other forms of prevention and for identification, reporting, referral, investigation, treatment and follow-up of instances of child maltreatment described heretofore, and, as appropriate, for judicial involvement.

The General Comment refers to other especially relevant articles (Article 5, direction and guidance consistent with evolving capacities; Article 9, separation from parents; Article 18, recognition and support of parental responsibilities; Article 27, adequate standard of living). Two Optional Protocols are particularly salient to the protection of children and prevention of violence: the Optional Protocol on the sale of children, child prostitution and child pornography; and the Optional Protocol on the involvement of children in armed conflict.[2]

The General Comment identifies an extensive range of forms of violence, from neglect to mental and physical violence, to violence through information and communication technologies, and self-harm. Using the term 'violence' rather than abuse (or child maltreatment), the General Comment presents a definition far wider than that commonly referred to within formal child protection guidance in the UK (e.g. see Scottish Government 2010).

There is emphasis on greater primary prevention, more comprehensive and reliable national and local data collection, improving interagency cooperation and families' important role (whilst recognising that much violence occurs in families). The General Comment seeks to maintain

---

2 Optional Protocols are additional legal mechanisms to the original treaty, which States must separately ratify for them to become legally binding. They are used for something further than the original treaty or to address new concerns. The official text of the UNCRC Optional Protocols can be found at www.ohchr.org/EN/HRBodies/CRC/Pages/CRCIndex.aspx.

children's place *in* childhood. For example, it makes explicit that *every* child has a caregiver: if the child lacks an obvious primary or proxy caregiver – for example, a child living on the street or children in a 'child-headed household' – then the state becomes the de facto caregiver (United Nations Committee on the Rights of the Child 2011, p.13). Children who are aggressive towards other children 'must be regarded as victims of their childrearing conditions' (United Nations Committee on the Rights of the Child 2011, p.20) and educated and supported rather than punished. Even if a person under the age of 18 has attained majority domestically, because of early marriage, the UN Committee seeks to apply Article 19 to them (United Nations Committee on the Rights of the Child 2011, p.12). The General Comment is thus spreading protection to the widest range of children, who might previously not have been considered legally, or treated by society and services, as children.

This spread risks 'returning' children to a traditional view of childhood, undermining children's agency and contributions and focusing solely on their vulnerability and developmental needs. But the UN Committee asserts they are taking a different approach: 'A child rights-based approach to child caregiving and protection requires a paradigm shift towards respecting and promoting the human dignity and the physical and psychological integrity of children as rights-bearing individuals rather than perceiving them primarily as "victims"' (United Nations Committee on the Rights of the Child 2011, p.3).

Thus, the UNCRC is seeking both to recognise the human dignity and capabilities of children and to protect them.

Critically considering the UNCRC

The UNCRC has been sharply criticised, alongside other international human rights treaties, for its claims to be universal, capable of being applied across all countries and contexts. In particular, the UNCRC has been accused of promoting a Minority World/Global North view of childhood, of emphasising children's lack of capacity, vulnerability, dependency, and place within nuclear families, which has damaging consequences for Majority World/Global South children, who do not fit that view (e.g. Ennew 1995; Wells 2009).

The assertion of individual children's rights, and specifically their right to be heard, have been described as being at odds with cultures that are more collective (Valentin and Meinert 2009). Such criticisms can be countered by recognising the openness of UNCRC interpretation and other human rights treaties: for example, the requirement to treat a child's best interests as a primary consideration (Article 3) leaves a great deal of national and local interpretation of what constitutes a child's best interests (see Alderson 2012; Burman 1996). Nonetheless, the proposed universality of children's rights, and their application in practice and in principle to the diversity of children cross-culturally, are some of the greatest challenges to and for the UNCRC and other human rights treaties.

Yet, rights do have particularly valuable 'moral coinage' (Freeman 1983, p.32) for those without other means of power. The moral coinage of rights, in the Minority World/Global North, arguably arises from the philosophy heritage of the Enlightenment period. Philosophers like John Locke (1982) sought to articulate the relationship between the individual citizen and the state, with concerns about legitimising and largely limiting state intervention in order to protect individuals' autonomy and freedoms. Rights were God-given and thus inalienable and universal (at least for adult men). Through the philosophical development of Liberal Theory, rights became 'political trumps' (Dworkin 1997, p.xi), claims that were non-negotiable and had to be met. As such, rights are 'the language of equality', writes McGillivray (1994, p.252), about 'dignity, respect, liberty, opportunities, access to and protection from the law, and participation in one's own fate'.

A rights-based approach has been contrasted to the traditional needs-based approach to children and their protection (e.g. Save the Children Sweden 2006). For example, a rights-based approach requires universal application to children rather than concern for the few, as in a needs-based approach; rights are indivisible and interdependent, and must be realised, whereas needs can be ranked in a hierarchy and thus prioritised. Power relationships are different: in a rights-based approach, beneficiaries are active participants in realising their rights and duty-bearers have responsibilities; whereas in a needs-based approach, beneficiaries are dependent on the powerful's goodwill and charity. While the comparison between needs and rights may lead to new insights, it leads to a mistaken idea that needs are not included within the UNCRC.

Article 3 (best interests), as well as the other range of Articles from health to education to play, are all arguably addressing children's needs; needs are *part* of the UNCRC but set within a rights framework (see Bessell and Gal 2009). Taking a rights-based approach, however, gives a different status to children and can be challenging to children's services (including formal child protection services) more used to focusing solely on children's and their families' needs (Tisdall and Davis 2015).

Rights, as they grew out of the Enlightenment and its Liberal Theory, though, have been accused of incorrectly perceiving society as formed from associational or contractual relationships based on mutual self-interests and such relationships being formed by individuals who are autonomous, rational and competent (e.g. Arneil 2002; Sandel 1982). A host of alternatives have been proposed, including recent interest in the alternative concept of 'vulnerability' (e.g. Fineman 2008, 2010/2011). Vulnerability recognises interdependence and relationships. Vulnerability arises because human beings have bodies and they have material needs, and thus all are exposed to threats of harm and privation. Fineman (2008) thus suggests vulnerability is useful because it is not exceptional but universal and constant. Individuals will differ in their range and magnitude of vulnerabilities but all people are vulnerable as part of the human condition. Society cannot eradicate vulnerability; rather it can and should mediate, compensate and lessen vulnerability. Vulnerability requires attention to and by the state, both in how it supports people and how it distributes social assets. This is thus a different state than the largely non-intervening one of Liberal Theory.

Herring (2012) finds vulnerability an attractive basis for children's law. Because everyone is vulnerable, Herring argues vulnerability avoids devaluing dependency and thus dependants. Rather than seeing vulnerability as negative, he perceives it as not only inevitable but welcome: 'Relationships; intimacy; care; all of these things in their nature render us vulnerable' (p.256). If the law acknowledged everyone was vulnerable, it would do away with the special 'concessions' in law for children or other 'vulnerable' adults. Instead, law and the legal system would take vulnerability as the norm and the focus would be on the special privileges given to able-bodied people or adults.

Vulnerability is a familiar term within child protection policy and practice, one that is widely and vaguely used. A common reference is made to 'vulnerable' populations, which almost inevitably include children and particular groups of children within that (Daniel 2010). Referring to 'the vulnerable' is not the empowering universality hoped for by Fineman and Herring but rather one that can be patronising and stigmatising and adds to social control (Brown 2011). As Daniel (2010) writes, the conceptualisation of children as 'vulnerable' weakens their claims to be heard, leading to professionals overriding children's wishes and ignoring children's contribution. Daniel's analysis draws attention to the problem of children, or any other 'vulnerable' group, leading the way in applying vulnerability theorisation. Because they are already placed in a marginalised position societally and legally, they risk being marginalised further by concentrating on vulnerability. It would require the wholesale reorientation of the state and law towards vulnerability, so that powerful groups within society were considered vulnerable, for the benefits of vulnerability to translate to a new position for children generally and in child protection particularly.

Conclusion

Children's rights have the potential, conceptually, to change perceptions of children. Rather than seeing children as 'the vulnerable', dependent victims, who need to be protected by the state based on their current needs and future wellbeing, children's rights conceptualise children as people who can make claims on duty-bearers, who can and do contribute to their families and communities and who are social actors in their own right.

Children's rights also have the potential, legally, to change the framing of child maltreatment – and how it is addressed. Protective approaches, write Reading and colleagues (2009), 'concentrate on legal and professional responses' (p.332), while public health approaches emphasise 'monitoring prevention, cost-effectiveness, and population strategies' (p.332). Children's rights, they continue, can bring together the best of both protective and public health approaches, while adding 'a legal instrument for implementing policy, accountability and social justice' (p.332). Reading and colleagues argue that a children's rights approach must include, but go beyond, a focus on individual harms to children by parents and other close adults (so much the focus of child protection systems in the Minority World/Global North) or on precise and limited definitions of intentional harm for public health monitoring.

For the UN to succeed, the focus needs to be on all violence against children, in a wider range of circumstances, and leaving no child out of its purview – from refugee and migrant children, to children on the street, to children who are involved in prostitution or early marriage. It will require agencies to work together and for prevention – including attention to socio-economic rights like an adequate standard of living – to be centralised and prioritised. Rather than child protection, we should be addressing the protection of children, bringing together the rights of protection, provision and participation.

A children's rights framework, however, has its disadvantages both conceptually and legally, as well as advantages. Conceptually, rights' political strength draws on Enlightenment-based, Liberal Theory that privileges the autonomous, rational (and adult) individual. Rights can fail to recognise the importance of love, relationships, community and networks; rights' claims to be universal can fail to be sensitive to different cultures and contexts. Yet the advantages of children's rights are considerable in creating a focus on children as part of human rights systems, as having status in their own right and on the necessity of recognising and supporting children's human dignity. Other alternatives like 'vulnerability' cannot do this. Children's rights need not be the only way to address or reconceptualise the protection of children (see Anderson and Honneth 2005) but a children's rights framework provides a particular contribution that suitably challenges the violence children continue to experience around the world.

CHAPTER 4

Armed Conflict and Political Violence

Jason Hart

Images and stories of children have been central to contemporary understanding of the horrors of war. Anne Frank's diary of life in Nazi-occupied Amsterdam (Frank 1947/2007), the photograph of Vietnamese Phan Thi Kim Phuc running naked from the site of a napalm attack, and Ishmael Beah's account of his experience as a boy soldier in Sierra Leone (Beah 2007), are among the familiar depictions of the brutality of contemporary warfare and of the particular suffering that the young are liable to endure.

In the wake of World War One, images of such suffering motivated a British woman, Eglantyne Jebb, to call upon the government to lift its blockade of central Europe so that the children of the defeated enemy would not continue to die of starvation (Mulley 2009). Ultimately, Jebb prevailed. Shortly afterwards she established Save the Children to institutionalise such efforts on behalf of children. The genesis of Save the Children illustrates the centrality of concern about protecting children[1] from the ill-effects of armed conflict[2] to broader aid efforts focused on the young.

---

1 In this chapter I use the term 'children' in line with the definition contained in the United Nations *Convention on the Rights of the Child* (1989) to refer to 'every human being below the age of 18 years'.

2 While recognising that 'political violence' might embrace a broader array of situations than 'armed conflict', in this chapter I use these two terms interchangeably.

The last two decades have witnessed an increase both in the scale and professionalisation of efforts by organisations such as Save the Children to address the harm to children resulting from political violence. Handbooks, training programmes, global standards, monitoring mechanisms, a plethora of publications by recognised experts and various resolutions of the United Nations (UN) attest to the emergence and importance of child protection as a discrete domain of humanitarian action. This field coheres around a definition of protection as actions intended to 'prevent and respond to violence, exploitation and abuse against children' (UNICEF 2006).

This chapter begins with reflection upon the specific protection needs of children in these settings as identified by child protection actors. I shall then consider the nature of the institutional response offered by organisations such as Save the Children. Particular attention will be paid to the challenges of public advocacy, given the political agendas and sensitivities attendant to many of the world's conflict zones. From such a perspective my chapter constitutes a call to consider child protection in a broader political-economic context. It concludes with an analysis of key ways in which this field requires further development if it is to ensure not just the healing of children harmed by political violence but also more effective prevention of such harm in the first instance.

Conceptualisation of threat

In settings of armed conflict and political violence the ways in which young people are rendered vulnerable to harm are specific and numerous. Aside from injury and death, serious violations can take the form of, *inter alia*: coerced recruitment to military groups; sexual and gender-based violence; denial of food and medical care; obstructions of access to education including through the targeted destruction of schools; and forced displacement tantamount to ethnic cleansing. Moreover, violations experienced by the young tend to be multiple and interrelated – a point not always reflected in the literature, which has often focused on single issues, such as military recruitment, in isolation (Bissell 2012, p.4).

Inevitably, forms of abuse and neglect conventionally addressed by social workers in non-conflict settings are also to be found in settings of political violence. Again, it is important to see how such threats to the young may be part of an interrelated web of protection concerns. For example, an increased rate of early marriage (of girls) in refugee camps and exploitative child labour are often attributed to the need of families fleeing conflict to reduce the burden on the household unit. Similarly, the pressures associated with life as a refugee or living amidst political violence have often been seen to result in heightened levels of domestic discord, even violence. This connection is not lost on young people themselves as this quote from a Palestinian girl indicates:

> Now if you experience the occupation, you have someone in prison or you don't know where they are [...] you will feel angry, stressed, you feel you cannot protect yourself; that will affect how you respond to the environment around you. So if my dad who's a taxi driver, if the soldiers take his ID or his driving licence, when he comes back home he will be angry and doesn't want to listen to us.[3]

The converse may also be true: abuse and neglect within the realm of family or community can result in young people engaging in political violence that renders them vulnerable to other sources of harm. This is illustrated by the following quote from a young female member of an armed group in Colombia:

> The day I got my uniform I understood that no one can harm me now. I have my weapons and I am very clever using them. I am the best in my battalion. My commander said that. And with my uniform everyone respects me, no man will dare to say dirty things in the pueblo to me. And my mother's boyfriend won't dare to touch me ever again.[4]

This quote prompts reflection upon the ways that the experience of abuse and neglect in their many forms might contribute to the emergence or perpetuation of political violence. Seeking to protect themselves from violations within the everyday settings of home and community, children may engage with military groups, thereby contributing to the continuation of armed conflict. Recognition of this dynamic entails questioning of the conventional wisdom that children are always coerced – through physical threat or brainwashing – into joining up with a military group.

---

3   14-year-old girl in focus group conducted by the author in the Nablus area of the West Bank in 2009. See Hart and Lo Forte (2010).

4   Unpublished. From author's communication with Laura Cordoba Bull, May 2006.

If we accept the proposition that an individual's capacity to connect the experience of oppression to larger societal structures can emerge *before* their 18th birthday, then it is possible to imagine that young people may be motivated to seek transformation of their situation through involvement in political violence. Indeed, numerous ethnographic accounts of specific conflict-affected locations indicate that young people's experience of injustice within everyday life can lead them to engage in various forms of combat (e.g. McIntyre 2005; Read 2001; Zharkevich 2009). Such a view contradicts the assumptions made in much of the advocacy-type literature about military recruitment: that all those under the age of 18, including teenagers, cannot be said to participate voluntarily in such activity since they lack the intellectual maturity to make social and political sense of their experience.

If young people are willing to risk their lives to transform, through violent means, a situation encountered as oppressive, then the conventional understanding of protection in emergency – as predicated on some version of Maslow's Pyramid of Human Needs (Maslow 1943) – is called into question. In my own ethnographic work with children in settings of political violence and in that of colleagues, the quest to secure human dignity for self or community has commonly emerged as an important priority for young people.

Yet, in Maslow's Pyramid such concerns are located towards the upper part – in the domains of esteem and self-actualisation – and are thus not considered primary. At the bottom are found physiological needs associated with survival and safety that are assumed to constitute universal priorities. The conceptual challenges of addressing the fact that for some young people the pursuit of dignity may take precedence over physical wellbeing are considerable. Assumptions of victimhood, of passivity and of inadequate comprehension by the young about the threats that they face may all require rethinking.

Institutional responses

Over recent years there have been increasing efforts by international non-governmental development organisations (INGDOs) and UN agencies to develop a multifaceted and integrated approach to child protection. Eschewing an 'issue by issue approach' that was often commonplace in child protection programming (Bissell 2012, p.1), considerable attention has been paid to the development of child protection systems that address threats (such as forced displacement and domestic violence) as interrelated (e.g. Terre des Hommes 2011; UNICEF 2013). Moreover, it has been asserted that a systems approach is likely to prove more cost effective and will also achieve a greater level of prevention of harm, balancing the often dominant focus on the response to harm already inflicted (Bissell 2012).

The 'protective environment framework' articulated by former UNICEF Chief of Child Protection Karin Landgren (2005) is an important example of such efforts to develop a coherent approach. As Landgren notes, agencies and donors concerned with child protection have tended to focus on one of two main areas: legal reform or service delivery (p.215). She argues instead for an approach that simultaneously embraces eight distinct areas. These relate to government commitment and capacity; legislation and enforcement; culture and customs; open discussion; children's life skills, knowledge and participation; capacity of families and communities; essential services; and monitoring, reporting and oversight (Landgren 2005, p.227).

Landgren acknowledges some of the particular challenges of protecting children in settings of armed conflict, given the common experience that 'the protective mechanisms of governance, policing and accountability break down and basic social services become sporadic or cease to be provided altogether' (p.225). However, her proposed framework is intended for general use across a range of settings and in relation to diverse threats to children's wellbeing. Although the protective environment framework has been utilised subsequently to address the protection needs of children living in settings of political violence (e.g. Ager, Boothby and Bremer 2008), reflection about the specific challenges of pursuing a systematic approach to protection work in such settings is arguably insufficient.

Institutional responses from humanitarian organisations have been developed largely under the rubric of either *child protection in emergencies* or *child protection in humanitarian action,* terms that not always helpfully elide so-called 'man-made' crises with 'natural' disasters (e.g. Child Protection Working Group 2013; Save the Children 2007). Although it is questionable whether humans, particularly powerful political-economic actors, are necessarily blameless for the latter[5], one evident consequence of labelling both as forms of emergency is to draw attention away from

---

5   For example, famine has often been seen to have both a natural and political-economic dimension. The Great Irish Famine in the mid-19th century is a case in point (Waters 1995).

the particular dynamics of humanitarian action amidst armed conflict. Here again, the specific challenges of working amidst political violence are not explicated adequately. The role of outside aid organisations in settings of political violence and the institutional considerations that are raised have been issues taken up most notably by Médecins Sans Frontières (Abu-Sada 2012; Magone, Neuman and Weissman 2011). However, comparable reflection on the institutional challenges of child protection work in such settings is still rare.

At the best of times an international or UN agency must negotiate a range of complex relationships – including to the host state, to local communities, to national elites and to donors – in defining and pursuing its objectives. However, in a setting of political violence such relationships are liable to be fraught with additional pressures and sensitivities. Far from being the principal guarantor of children's rights to protection, as envisaged by the UN *Convention on the Rights of the Child* (UNCRC, United Nations 1989), host governments are often responsible for immense and systematic violations.

The Assad regime in Syria, the Sudanese authorities in Darfur and the generals ruling Burma are a few of the most obvious examples of governments whose actions put the lives of many children on their sovereign territory at risk. Understandably, national leaders responsible for violations are keen to avoid the negative publicity resulting from public statements by child protection organisations that could damage their international standing. Thus, for example, while protesting about the recruitment of children by rebel groups, authorities may take a harsh line with any organisation seeking to address such involvement by the young in their own forces. This is a situation familiar to humanitarians working in Sri Lanka, for example, during that country's recent civil war. Here the government, engaged in a long-running civil war with the separatist Liberation Tigers of Tamil Elam (LTTE), routinely decried the latter's use of children in military roles while seeking to obscure its own use of the young through armed 'home guard' units and its support of allied Tamil paramilitary groups that routinely employed children (see BBC 1999; Human Rights Watch 2006).

Challenging governments over their violations entails risk. In many settings child protection actors must weigh up the need to undertake public advocacy with the need to continue delivery of services on the ground. This was a situation that I encountered in Bhutan in 2001 when conducting research across South Asia on the impact of armed conflict on children. At that time the regime refused to entertain any discussion of its violent crackdown on the Nepali-speaking population in the south and its efforts to compel emigration. For the most part the heads of development and humanitarian agencies present in the capital, Thimpu, spoke in hushed voices about the violations, including the denial of Nepali-speaking children's access to formal education, for fear of being thrown out of the country. A notable exception was the head of one organisation, who argued that it might be preferable to risk expulsion – and thereby bring global public attention to the situation – rather than remain silent and become complicit as a result. This divergence of opinion illustrates the specific dilemmas that child protection organisations may encounter in settings of political violence and the role of individual and institutional political will.

In addition to the pressure from host governments, humanitarians must negotiate the agendas of donors. Agencies such as UNICEF and Save the Children usually rely heavily on funds from Western governments for their child protection work in conflict-affected settings. By contrast, natural disasters such as the 2006 Indian Ocean Tsunami often attract huge contributions from citizens. All humanitarian activity, including child protection programming, can become subject to the particular scrutiny of the donor government's ministry of foreign affairs when pursued in regions where that government has strong interests.

I have witnessed the influence upon actions, and inactions, on the ground resulting from donor agendas, most explicitly in the occupied Palestinian territory (oPt)[6], a location in which I have studied, worked as a teacher and conducted research over a period of 20 years. My most recent research was in 2009–10 when, together with Claudia Lo Forte, I produced a study on the role of international organisations in protecting Palestinian children from the violence associated with Israel's occupation of the West Bank and East Jerusalem (Hart and Lo Forte 2010).

Here the political stakes are especially high. Leaders are faced with the demands of powerful interest groups – most notably the pro-Israel lobby (which in the US includes fundamentalist Christian groups), and the arms, security and oil industries (Cronin 2010; Mearsheimer and Walt 2007). Little wonder, then, that organisations relying on the support of the US, Canada, Australia, the European Union (EU) or individual European states should be placed under pressure not to

6 The term 'occupied Palestinian territory' – as employed by the UN and the International Committee of the Red Cross – refers to land conquered in the war of 1967 and since occupied. This territory comprises East Jerusalem, Gaza, the West Bank and part of the Golan Heights.

speak too loudly or too critically about violations routinely visited by
the Israeli authorities and settlers on Palestinian children (Hart and Lo
Forte 2013). In the words of a Palestinian social work scholar whom
Claudia and I interviewed in 2009:

> It's a political protection. I mean everyone knows this,
> even donors. I never met a donor who doesn't know this.
> But they are constrained. All of them would talk off the
> record. They all are constrained. They all understand the
> imbalance of power that is the source of all the problems
> [...] but they have their jobs, they work within their
> mandates. (Hart and Lo Forte 2013, p.638)

In highlighting the pressures and constraints on child protection
organisations my intention is not to suggest that all efforts at programming
are doomed to failure or, at the least, to serious compromise. That would
be an overstatement. Rather I seek to draw attention to the specificity of
such efforts in the context of political violence where the agendas to be
negotiated exist not just at the local or national level but internationally as
well. This is an issue rarely discussed openly by the agencies themselves.
Yet, I would argue, without awareness of these dynamics we cannot fully
comprehend how child protection is pursued, or not, on the ground.
This can be illustrated, for example, in the way that the duty to be
accountable to beneficiaries is discharged.

Amongst practitioners and scholars of development and
humanitarianism, accountability is commonly viewed as a core element
of a rights-based approach (Cornwall and Nyamu-Musembi 2004),
particularly so-called 'downwards accountability' to the local population
(Ebrahim 2003). In settings of political violence, however, engaging
with a local population to identify and act in accordance with their
aspirations – in this case for the protection of the young – is fraught
with difficulty and risk for the agencies themselves.

Leaving aside the practicalities of achieving community-wide
agreement about priorities, the space for response to those priorities will
clearly be constrained by the demands of donors and host states. How,
for example, should organisations respond when local people call upon
them to speak out about the need to remove Jewish extremists who

have settled on their land in violation of international law?[7] When, as has happened in the South Hebron Hills, settlers threaten children on their way to and from school and prevent the development of basic infrastructure including the provision of piped water, what should be the response of agencies mandated to protect children? (Beinin 2007; Zertal and Eldar 2005.)[8]

Action in response to the demands of parents for protective intervention or advocacy would potentially place the agency in a vulnerable position with its funders and with the state responsible – in this case Israel.[9]

Not surprisingly, in settings of such geopolitical sensitivity as Israel/oPt the kind of discussions between outside agencies and local communities focused on the design, monitoring and evaluating of interventions seen in many other aid contexts are few and far between. Moreover, for all the rhetoric of children's participation in programmatic activities, in such settings engagement with the young must be managed carefully if humanitarian organisations are not to be presented with a set of priorities for which they would not wish to render themselves accountable (see Hart 2012, p.483).

The kind of institutional considerations that might constrain the manner in which accountability and advocacy are pursued can also be seen to inform the nature of protection programming itself. An abundance of 'psychosocial programming' is commonplace in many settings of political violence. The term 'psychosocial' covers a wide range of activities: from playgroups to individual counselling. Although it is not always seen formally as an aspect of protection programming, in practice this work can constitute a major, if not the primary, domain of activity for humanitarian organisations working to protect the young.

---

7 Security Council Resolution 446 (1979) affirms that the transfer of Jewish settlers into the oPt constitutes a violation of the Fourth Geneva Convention. See http://unispal.un.org/UNISPAL.NSF/0/BA123CDED3EA84A5852560E50077C2DC.

8 For further information about the attacks on children by settlers in the South Hebron Hills, see the website of the Christian Peacemakers Team www.cpt.org/cptnet/2014/04/09/tuwani-military-escort-misconduct-exposes-palestinian-children-risk-their-way-and-.

9 Landgren (2005) cites the report of a workshop on rights-based approaches held by Save the Children Sweden in 2003 where 'one of the main criticisms was that development actors in general were seen to refrain from pressurising governments about specific rights violations, for fear of risking their legitimacy and future programme activities' (p.224).

For example, according to their website the child protection work of the US branch of Save the Children International operating in the oPt consists entirely of psychosocial programming intended to provide, in that organisation's words, 'a lifeline for children at risk'.[10] My recent fieldwork looking at the institutional response to Iraqi refugees in Jordan revealed a similar preponderance of psychosocial programming in a setting where the closure of resettlement programmes, the denial of access to the formal labour market and the withdrawal of cash support for impoverished families were exerting a wholly negative effect on the capacity of primary caregivers to protect the young (Hart and Kvittingen 2015). As in the oPt, the aim of psychosocial programming seemed to be to strengthen the refugees' ability to cope with intolerable circumstances in part occasioned by institutional neglect.

The scale of psychosocial programming can be partly explained as a function of the central role of mental health experts in the development of child protection work in emergencies. However, it is also institutionally expedient. Focusing on psycho-emotional needs draws attention away from political-economic forces that commonly give rise to threats to the wellbeing of young people and about which, in my experience, they often have much to say. In the Palestinian context, children and youth have worked collectively to produce their own set of demands from the international community – demands that many outside humanitarian agencies would be nervous of taking on.

For example, in 2002, members of the 'Young Parliament' of 9–15-year-olds in Gaza, working under the auspices of the Cana'an Institute, created a petition that called upon the international community to fulfil its obligations for their protection. This petition was signed by 20,000 Palestinian children and delivered to Mary Robinson, then UN High Commissioner for Human Rights, during her visit to Gaza.[11] It is far safer for an organisation, anxious not to alienate the host government or major donors, to engage with the young in the context of psychosocial activities – as either 'traumatised' or 'resilient' – than to open up discussion predicated on recognition of them as social actors with aspirations to live with dignity, free of routine violations.

---

10 See: www.savethechildren.org/site/c.8rKLIXMGIpI4E/b.6153151/k.5AE1/West_Bank_and_Gaza_Strip.htm.

11 See also the 'Gazan Youth's Manifesto for Change' at www.theguardian.com/world/2011/jan/02/free-gaza-youth-manifesto-palestinian.

Moving forward

The call by former UNICEF Chief of Child Protection Karin Landgren (2005) and her successor Susan Bissell (2012) for an integrated, systematic approach to child protection is unquestionably important to heed. However, for this to become achievable in many of the locations around the globe currently afflicted by political violence, consideration is needed of the larger system within which such an approach is pursued. Child protection organisations are unavoidably implicated in this larger system through their relationship to host states, major donors and fellow agencies. In situations of political violence the interests of these different actors are likely to be pronounced, relating to goals around political gain, institutional survival and the management of public relations, which may be incompatible with a prevention-focused approach to child protection.

On the face of it, international law appears to offer tools to challenge governments involved in the systematic violation of children's rights. There is no shortage of legal instruments from International Humanitarian Law, Human Rights Law and Refugee Law that might be utilised to bring violators to account, with new legal measures such as the 'Model Child Protection Law' under development (see The Protection Project and ICMEC 2013). However, the challenge lies in implementation.

On the one hand, child protection organisations need to build their own understanding of, and ability to utilise, legal instruments. With the notable exception of an online training programme developed by UNICEF, efforts to develop such capacity have been limited (UNICEF 2004). On the other hand, debate is needed about the constraints and opportunities for an agency to invoke international law as a meaningful part of its work. What are the limitations of the current system and how might these be overcome through concerted action?

In recent years there have been numerous statements made by leading child protection organisations about the foundational nature of international law for child protection work, but little has been suggested about actual use (e.g. Bissell 2011). This includes the new *Minimum Standards for Child Protection in Humanitarian Action,* which, as the authors explain, 'are grounded in an international legal framework that regulates the obligations of the State towards its citizens and other persons in that State' (Child Protection Working Group 2013, p.14). Yet the 256 page document offers no guidance on how the framework might be put into service for the protection of children, let alone how to meet the challenges in attempting to do so.

Exploring these issues inevitably entails acknowledgement of the larger political-economic forces within which organisations such as UNICEF, Save the Children and others operate.

Throughout this chapter I have spoken only of the UN and international agencies working on child protection in settings of political violence. In practice, however, much of the work on the ground is conducted by local organisations. Although commonly referred to as 'partnership', in reality relationships between UN agencies/INGDOs and local organisations are often riven with hierarchy. The former hold the funds, albeit on behalf of donors, and the latter are commonly obliged to operate in line with the plans and wishes coming from above in the manner of a subcontractor rather than a genuine partner.

Such hierarchy serves to prevent dialogue that might bring into regular view realities on the ground and thereby help to promote awareness of the larger system. At the risk of overgeneralisation, local agencies, working closer to the affected communities and staffed less by national elites, are generally more aware than the INGDOs and UN agencies of the dynamics that render the young vulnerable to violations in the context of political violence.

Brought meaningfully into the design and evaluation of programming, the experience of local organisations could help to ensure the greater relevance and efficacy of protection work and go some way to address the imperative to pursue 'downwards accountability'. However, the obstacles to such dialogue are numerous. The institutional global architecture of child protection, which places the UN in a central coordination role, donor agendas, and the quasi-colonial terms of engagement that commonly shape so-called 'partnership' between UN agencies/INGDOs and local organisations are some of the main challenges here. It is my contention that the better protection of children living amidst political violence depends on overcoming these obstacles as well.

Conclusion

In this chapter I have sought to identify some of the key child protection concerns arising in the context of political violence. In doing so, I cautioned against assuming necessary universality around the prioritisation of these concerns. The implicit message is that engagement in open-ended dialogue with affected populations, including the young themselves, is vital to ensure that threats and protection needs are properly understood. This would be the ideal.

My subsequent discussion of organisational response indicated some of the systemic obstacles to the realisation of a more engaged, dialogic way of working in settings of political violence. While the rights-based approach nominally pursued by most aid organisations working on child protection includes the principle of accountability to local populations, in reality larger institutional considerations make this a risky endeavour. In consequence, as seems evident in various settings of political violence around the world, agencies pursue child protection in ways that reflect principle only in so far as it is expedient to do so.

According to the text of the UNCRC (1989, Article 3) 'in all actions concerning children […] the best interests of the child shall be a primary consideration'[12]. Why this may often not be the case in child protection work and how the obstacles preventing primary attention to the best interests principle can be overcome are topics that merit urgent debate amongst practitioners and policy makers.

---

12 www.ohchr.org/en/professionalinterest/pages/crc.aspx.

PART 2

Challenge Two: Reviewing the Evidence

CHAPTER 5

The Ethics of Predictive Risk Modelling

Tim Dare

Introduction

The opportunity to have an early and accurate assessment of the likelihood that a child will be the victim of maltreatment in the future promises obvious benefits.

Recent research suggests that predictive risk models – automated tools that gather and process information held in existing datasets in order to determine patterns and predict future outcomes – go at least some way towards making such assessments possible.

However the application of predictive risk modelling (PRM) to child maltreatment brings ethical risks and costs, including the possible stigmatisation of already vulnerable populations, predictable false positives (the incorrect classification of families as high risk), the use of data without consent, difficulties in designing and implementing effective interventions, and resource allocation issues. Not surprisingly, predictive tools have been treated with suspicion in the child welfare area (Munro 2007).

This chapter takes a predictive risk model developed in New Zealand (the Vulnerable Children PRM), as its focus and attempts to identify and respond to at least some of the ethical risks associated with the use of PRM in child protection, suggesting that the ethical costs associated with such modelling can be addressed or ameliorated or are outweighed by its potential benefits.

The Vulnerable Children PRM

The Vulnerable Children PRM (Vaithianathan *et al*. 2012, 2013) was developed and validated using an anonymised dataset linking administrative records from New Zealand's welfare benefit and Child, Youth and Family Services systems for children who were born between January 2003 and June 2006 and had a benefit spell before the age of two: a sample of 57,986 children comprising about 33 per cent of all children born in New Zealand during that period.

The PRM algorithm was developed by identifying potential variables in cases of substantiated maltreatment in 70 per cent of the sample. 132 variables – including demographic and historical features of a child, their family, household and community – were found to make a statistically significant contribution to the model and were therefore retained in a 'core algorithm' which was tested on the remaining 30 per cent validation sample. The algorithm generated a risk decile score at the start of each new benefit spell for each child in the sample with 10 indicating a child as being within the top 10 per cent of risk, down to 1 as being in the bottom 10 per cent.[1]

By their fifth birthday, 48 per cent of children in the validation sample with a risk score of 10, and 29 per cent with a risk score of 9, had a substantiated maltreatment finding, compared with around 2 per cent of children with the lowest risk score.[2]

Of all New Zealand children, 5.4 per cent have a substantiated maltreatment finding by age five; 83 per cent of those children would have appeared in the project sample (that is, started a benefit spell before age two), and so received a risk score under the proposed algorithm.

The researchers suggested focusing intensive intervention on children with risk scores of 9 and 10. This would involve offering intensive intervention to 5 per cent of the total population, with a false

---

1 The algorithm recognises dynamic risk factors; it produces a risk score at the start of any new benefit spell that occurred before the child's second birthday. A new spell starts whenever the benefit system records alterations in a family's circumstances indicated by changes such as a change of benefit type, the arrival or departure of a partner, or movement of a child from one caregiver to another.

2 The Receiver Operating Characteristic curve is commonly used as a more thorough indication of a predictive model's accuracy. The Area Under the Curve (AUC) indicates the accuracy of a model. For comparison's sake, a perfect predictive model, which gives all and only true positives and true negatives, would receive a 100 per cent AUC, while a model that can discern a true positive or negative no better or worse than chance would receive a 50 per cent AUC. The AUC for this model is approximately 76 per cent, which is technically regarded as fair, approaching good.

positive rate of 63 per cent and capture rate of 37 per cent of national maltreatment cases. If intervention were offered to all 9 or 10 risk score cases, and 50 per cent took up the offer, 280 cases of maltreatment of children under five would be prevented for every two years of the programme, assuming a nominal prevention-per-intervention rate of 46 per cent.[3]

The power of the Vulnerable Children PRM is obviously central to an ethical evaluation of its implementation. I do not review the grounds for confidence in the model in this chapter: they are presented in more detail in Viathianathan *et al.* 2012, 2013. The AVC for the model (see Footnote 2) is similar to that for a mammogram conducted without prior risk indication of cancer – as is done in New Zealand.

Instead I accept, *arguendo*, that the model is as described and so begin from the assumption that PRM has the potential to deliver very considerable benefits in the child protection area. It may seem that this assumption begs the crucial question, assuming at the outset the very issue at the heart of an ethical analysis of PRM. I hope it will become clear that in fact the assumption leaves most of the key ethical issues open: issues concerning false positives, stigmatisation, the preference for targeted over universal responses and constraints on ethical screening programmes.

PRMs and Actuarial Risk Assessment (ARA) tools

It seems likely that at least some opposition to the use of PRM in child protection flows from experience with alternative predictive tools, most commonly 'operator driven' Actuarial Risk Assessment (ARA) tools.

ARAs have well-recognised weaknesses. They are rarely validated for the populations to which they are applied, undermining efficacy in the face of variations across geographies and child welfare populations, and are dependent on trained and motivated frontline social workers or other agents to apply them and to respond to the estimated risk, workers who do not always use them in the way that policy makers or designers envisaged (Broadhurst *et al.* 2010; Gillingham and Humphreys 2010). Automated PRMs avoid at least some of the problems that have undermined confidence in ARAs. In contrast to ARAs, PRMs require no manual data entry, instead using routinely collected administrative data

---

3   These figures are derived from the US Nurse Family Partnership Programme, used in Vaithianathan *et al.* (2012) as an illustration of possible intervention models. See Olds (2006).

to exploit historical correlations and patterns for a specific population. Their reliance upon specific datasets makes it more likely that they will be validated for populations, or even for specific subsets of populations. They can process vastly larger sets of data than operator-driven alternatives, and so offer dramatically more accurate risk assessments.

PRM and child protection: ethical issues
Needles in haystacks

Some critics have argued that the use of automated prediction and surveillance tools in child protection may be positively harmful – in part, because they fear such tools might overwhelm services with referrals. Eileen Munro (2007, p.52) writes:

> The basic problem is that by magnifying the amount of data being collected so much, there is a risk that cases of serious abuse will be hidden in the deluge of data about lower level concerns. [...] The UK Information Commissioner [...] summed up the problem: 'When you are looking for a needle in a haystack I am not sure it is wise to make the haystack bigger.

However this concern seems only indirectly or contingently relevant to PRM and the information and communication technologies Munro has in mind in her discussion. Strategies that required police to refer every domestic violence incident in households with children were low-tech, but created the same difficulties. The 'needle in a haystack' problem is one that arises for a wide range of referral strategies. Whether it is a problem for PRM will depend upon contingent implementation strategies, including, for instance, decisions around thresholds for referral. From this perspective, it is hard not to think that there is a curious assumption behind the haystack metaphor: if we *know* there are needles in the haystack, we can take no comfort from restricting the scope of the search. We need better needle detectors. A risk stratification tool that sorted cases by risk might go some way to addressing that need.

Similar points can be made in response to other common criticisms of PRM. It has been suggested, for instance, that such technology will lead child protection workers to trust their computers rather than their own judgement and lead to the loss of universal child protection policies. But again there is nothing in PRM that entails these sorts of results. Such a system need not – an important implementation suggestion in the New Zealand case was that it must not – replace child protection workers or diminish the role for their judgement or engagement with clients[4] or replace universal child support.

A key component of recommendations about implementation in the New Zealand case was the creation or maintenance of alternative routes of referral. With respect to some of these concerns, one might hope it would have the opposite effect. Many ARAs relied upon child protection workers to identify, record and report risk factors. Better, one might think, to leave the complex and time-consuming data collection and validation tasks to an automated system and its designers (properly informed by social workers), freeing frontline staff to exercise experience and judgement in decisions about the proper response to validated risk assessments delivered by the tool.

My point is not that these are not legitimate concerns about child protection policies. It is rather that they should not be seen as having particular force against PRM or similar tools. They impact equally upon a range of child protection policies, and, if we entertain the possibility that PRM might be a valuable tool, they are best seen as reasons to implement PRM in some ways rather than others.

Universal versus targeted responses

I have suggested that the introduction of PRM does not require the reduction of existing universal services, but there are a number of other ethical issues around the distinction between universal and targeted services, and in particular a number of reasons not to rely solely upon universal services.

New Zealand already offers universal assistance to families but there is little reason to think those programmes will address New Zealand's child maltreatment problem if maintained at their current levels of intensity; after all, they are already in place and available to all New Zealand families. There are also reasons to be wary of making

---

4   See for instance the New Zealand *White Paper for Vulnerable Children* (2012) Volume II, p.80: 'Predicting maltreatment is not easy, and risk scoring will be just one component of a wider system to target support to vulnerable children [...] Children who are not picked up by the model will still be able to be identified as at risk and prioritised for assessment and services through identification by frontline professionals, including care and protection social workers'. Available at www.msd.govt.nz/documents/about-msd-and-our-work/work-programmes/policy-development/white-paper-vulnerable-children/whitepaper-volume-ii-web.pdf, accessed on 12 May 2015.

the existing universal programmes more intensive. It might be difficult, for instance, to maintain the important existing relationships between families and the nurses and community health workers who deliver current universal services while changing their focus and intensity: it may matter that the existing services are relatively light-touch. Further, universal programmes are expensive, and they would be even more so if made more intensive.

Given the relatively low incidence of serious child maltreatment, much of these added costs would be directed to families whose children were not at elevated risk of maltreatment. For these families, there would be no gain in terms of reduced maltreatment outcomes from resources directed to them. However, such an allocation would mean that fewer resources would be available to treat families whose children were at elevated risk. Intensive programmes also impose costs on targeted families.

Even in the case of families identified as high risk, intervention should be moderated to reduce those burdens, especially since we know some will be incorrectly identified as at risk. That same argument would apply in the case of a universal programme, but in that case with no reason for thinking the burdens of such intervention were warranted at the outset.

Stigmatisation

The possible stigmatisation of risk-scored individuals and families is a particularly troubling potential cost of PRM. There are a number of aspects to the problem. The burdens associated with identification as an at-risk individual or group may increase the risk of the predicted adverse outcome, increasing pressure on already struggling families, reducing their readiness to engage with service providers and leading professionals to engage differently with stigmatised individuals. The burdens that follow from being identified as a member of a group often rest on false beliefs about what membership means, but while such stigmatisation is ill-founded, it is no less onerous for those who bear it. Policy makers who trigger such costs must take them into account, even though they may think them completely without foundation and even though the policy makers are at most only indirectly responsible for their imposition on the bearers of illegitimate stigma.[5] The burdens of stigmatisation, furthermore, often fall upon those who are already the subject of social disapproval or demarcation, 'appropriating and reinforcing pre-existing stigma' (Parker and Aggleton 2002).

Inevitably, beneficiaries will be overrepresented in the high-risk deciles generated by the Vulnerable Children PRM even if the data available to the model's algorithm is broadened beyond that in the welfare and CYF (Child Youth and Family) databases. A recent New Zealand Human Rights Commission report showed high levels of discrimination against beneficiaries (Dickison 2013), echoing the results of a similar study in the UK (Baumberg et al. 2012). These pre-existing vulnerabilities and stigmas clearly raise a particular ethical duty of care when considering action that may exacerbate the social disapproval and isolation already experienced by groups and individuals.

The most obvious way to reduce or eliminate stigmatisation is to maintain careful control over the dissemination of the 'product' of the PRM. It is, of course, not possible to obtain the benefits of PRM without at-risk families being identified at some point. If intensive services are to be targeted, those in high-risk groups must be identified to at least service providers. Such information, however, should be disseminated as narrowly as possible, in a way that is consistent with achieving the benefits of the programme and only with the level of detail required to make effective use of the model's predictions. Other consequences might be addressed by ensuring that intervention is supportive and preventative, rather than punitive. This focus is appropriate in any event, since not only will a significant portion of families not go on to record maltreatment findings, none of the families need to have done so at the time at which they appear in the Vulnerable Children PRM's risk rankings.

Responses must not prejudge individuals or families or appear to do so. Carefully ensuring that services are supportive and preventive may also increase the acceptability and so the effectiveness of engagement. Risk classifications should be expressed in ways that do not suggest that wrongdoing has occurred. The authors of a European study of early prediction and risk detection models in child protection follow this line of reasoning to conclude that while labelling families as 'high

---

5 Stigmatisation will not always be driven by 'beliefs' and this may matter. Racism, for instance, is likely to be significantly grounded in sub-doxastic (i.e. non-belief-driven) states or unreflective emotions not easily corrected through education.

risk' would be unethical and stigmatising, given the modest power of the tools they were considering (all considerably less precise than the Vulnerable Children PRM), nonetheless screening to identify children and families in need of more support was justified, provided the classification of families was expressed positively, as, for instance, 'high priority for services' rather than 'high risk' (Browne and Chou n.d.).

Child protection professionals must be trained to avoid confirmation bias insofar as it is possible to do so. Such bias is notoriously difficult to counter, but perhaps PRM could help. It is more rigid and transparent than any of our internalised heuristics about 'what sort of people' are more likely to be at risk, and so may act as a yardstick against which child protection officials can test their preconceptions.

Ethical preconditions for screening

It is widely recognised that despite their capacity to deliver considerable benefits, allowing efficient allocation of resources and early diagnosis and intervention, screening programmes also carry some costs, including those associated with the burdens of compliance, over-diagnosis, misdiagnosis and the creation of anxiety or unwarranted confidence.

The World Health Organization (WHO) lists ten prerequisites to be met by any ethical screening programme (Wilson and Jungner 1968); Lewis *et al.* (2013) suggest that equivalent caveats should apply to a PRM approach to stratifying a population according to their risk. I focus here on the WHO's Principle 2 (described by Wilson and Jungner (1968) as 'perhaps the most important') and its PRM analogue – the idea that in order for screening to be ethical there should be 'a treatment for the condition' or 'an intervention that can mitigate the risk of the event'.

This is not because we do not want to know about needs that are genuine but cannot be met. We may be able to meet them in the future, and knowing about them may provide an incentive to improve our capacity to help. Rather, the availability of an effective intervention is a prerequisite to an ethical screening programme because the screening process or some set of responses to it may themselves be potentially harmful and hence require the possibility of a countervailing benefit.

Evidence of the efficacy of available child maltreatment interventions is *arguably* sufficient to satisfy Principle 2. A handful of programmes, including the Nurse Family Partnership programme, used to calculate possible effects of the Vulnerable Children PRM (Olds *et al.* 1997)[6] – have shown some evidence of capacity to reduce child maltreatment. Furthermore, while meta-analyses of child maltreatment interventions emphasise the sparse and mixed nature of the evidence that they reduce the 'direct measures' (Mikton and Butchart 2009, p.354) of child maltreatment, there is greater confidence that they contribute indirectly to that goal.

Mikton and Butchart (2009) conclude that meta-reviews of intervention programmes 'suggest that early home visitation programmes are effective in reducing risk factors for child maltreatment, but whether they reduce direct measures is less clear-cut' (p.354). According to Howard and Brooks-Gunn (2009, p.134), 'the evidence…is stronger with respect to parenting and the quality of the home environment [than with respect to maltreatment]' and that 'home visits impart positive benefits to families by way of influencing maternal parenting practices, the quality of the child's environment and children's development' (p.119). Even if intervention with high-risk families cannot be proven *directly* to reduce the risk of maltreatment, then there does seem reason to think that appropriate interventions may be effective against a broader range of conditions plausibly related to maltreatment risk. If this is right, there is reason to think that the Vulnerable Children PRM meets the requirements of WHO's ethical screening Principle 2 and its PRM analogue.

Over-and-under identification

All PRMs will make some errors at any threshold for referral, identifying as low risk some children who go on to experience abuse or neglect and identifying as high risk some children who do not. One obvious response to the issue of false negatives is to broaden the databases upon which the Vulnerable Children PRM draws.

Currently, families who do not have contact with New Zealand's welfare or child support agencies' umbrella will not appear in the

---

6   The Nurse Family Partnership is a US home visiting programme for first-time low-income mothers. It was evaluated in three pilot demonstration sites and has replicated many positive effects on children's development, but it was possible to test its impact on substantiated maltreatment reports in one site only. Nonetheless, Mikton and Butchart (2009) identify the Nurse Family Partnership in the US 'as the only home visiting programme whose effectiveness has been unambiguously demonstrated. A randomized controlled trial showed a 48% reduction in actual child abuse at 15-year follow-up'.

databases available to the tool. They may appear in other databases, however, such as those generated by the health system and the births, deaths and marriages registry. As already suggested, we should also ensure that other routes of referral are created or maintained. These responses – broadening the databases available to the Vulnerable Children PRM and maintaining alternative referral routes – are essentially efforts to provide as broad and accurate a referral process as possible.

As regards to false positives – the incorrect classification of families as high risk – one should reduce the false-positive rate, for example by choosing higher thresholds for intervention. Beyond this, one might reduce the ethical significance of false positives in the child maltreatment context by reducing the significance of the consequences of misidentification. Some ways to do that include:

- providing opportunity for experienced child protection professionals to exercise judgement about appropriate responses to a family's identification as at risk

- ensuring that such professionals understand the potential of the Vulnerable Children PRM to miscategorise families

- providing training to guard, insofar as possible, against confirmation bias in the professional engagement with families identified as high risk

- offering rather than requiring engagement as a consequence of identification as at risk

- ensuring that intervention triggered by identification as at risk is as non-intrusive as possible, consistent with the overall aims of reducing child maltreatment risk

- ensuring that intervention triggered by identification, as at risk is positive and supportive rather than punitive, and identifying and minimising the adverse effects of identification as at risk, such as, possible stigmatisation.

Privacy and rights

PRM clearly raises significant issues around privacy and confidentiality. Although the two are interrelated it is useful to maintain the distinction since they pick out two rather different sets of concerns. Confidentiality is concerned with data or information and its security. My doctor is required to keep my health information confidential; she may not pass it on to others without my consent. Privacy need not involve information or the threat that it might be misused.

PRIVACY

If people have moral rights to privacy, then the Vulnerable Children PRM may pose ethical risks not remedied by, for instance, controlling the dissemination of information or ensuring that interventions pose as little burden as possible. The breach of such rights consists not of the collection or misuse of information, or the imposition of costs, but of the trespass itself. However, there are reasons to be wary of an absolute moral right to privacy, particularly in (for instance, domestic) contexts in which such rights have the capacity to shield domination, degradation and abuse. It seems unlikely that one should think privacy a knockdown reason to reject the implementation of PRM in child protection.

CONFIDENTIALITY

The Vulnerable Children PRM raises clear confidentiality issues insofar as it generates risk predictions by drawing from databases that hold information gathered for purposes other than child protection, which will be accessed (almost certainly) without the consent or knowledge of those who supplied that information.

We should put aside one potential response at the outset. Standard welfare application forms often include notice that information is being collected, for instance, in order to provide for the 'care and protection needs of children'.[7] It might be tempting to rely on such clauses as indicating there has been consent to the use of that information by child protection PRMs. But applicants are unlikely to feel they have a genuine real choice about whether to accept the conditions: they may be seeking essential support for themselves and their children and are hardly in a position to haggle over terms. And even if we accept that those filling out such forms have consented to have their information used to provide for the 'care and protection needs of children', it would not follow that they had consented to have their information used for the purposes of a predictive risk model.

What, then, if we assume that consent is lacking? An initial question is just what sort of disclosure is being contemplated? The

---

7 See, for instance, New Zealand's SDE Parent Support Application: www. workandincome.govt.nz/documents/forms/sole-parent-support-application.pdf, (p.32).

more detail disclosed and the wider the disclosure, the greater the confidentiality issues.

I have already suggested that disclosure of information generated by the Vulnerable Children PRM should be as narrow as possible, consistent with achieving the important moral goals of the tool. A similar approach might be taken towards the *content* of the information disclosed. We can imagine a range of possibilities: protection workers might be provided with full details of a family's circumstances, including the risk ranking, and if the tool is able to provide it, details of changes in circumstances that have triggered revised rankings.

Towards the other end of the range of possibilities, we might imagine child protection officials receiving *only* a list of names of those who appear in the highest risk deciles, without further information from the tool. Under this latter approach, child protection professionals would be called upon to initiate an assessment of the circumstances of the family, in order to determine what action should be taken. Any information that was uncovered by the assessment would be generated by activities identical to those used in current social work practice, the only difference being that the process was initiated by the Vulnerable Children PRM rather than by a health worker, social worker or member of the public.

It is common for confidentiality (or information privacy) protocols to allow for exceptions and limitations. The duties of confidentiality under the Code of Ethics of New Zealand Social Workers' hold, for instance, *subject to* emergencies 'in which it is in the client's best interests' or 'where the client or someone else (such as a child) may be endangered or harmed by non-disclosure'.[8] In hard cases, at least, one simply cannot apply such clauses without weighing the duty of confidentiality against other important competing interests.

There is also a more pragmatic concern about confidentiality, which is often defended on the consequentialist grounds that without a more-or-less absolute guarantee, clients would not engage with professionals or give accurate information. The force of this sort of argument is clear in cases in which clients or patients are deciding whether to give clearly culpatory information – the patient must decide whether to tell the GP the truth about their child's injury; the client must decide whether to tell their lawyer about their foreign bank account – but it is

---

8   The Code of Ethics of the Aotearoa New Zealand Association of Social Workers, para. 3.13. Available at http://anzasw.org.nz/documents/0000/0000/0664/ Chapter_3_Code_of_Ethics_Summary.pdf, accessed on 12 May 2015.

less obvious how the argument applies to the sort of administrative data upon which PRMs rely.

Conclusion

This chapter has attempted to identify and respond to at least some of the ethical risks associated with the use of PRM in child protection. My starting point – no doubt shared by all the contributors to this discussion – is that there is a powerful ethical imperative to find a way to protect the most vulnerable members of our community. While the application of PRM to child maltreatment does raise significant ethical concerns, I have suggested they can either be significantly mitigated by appropriate implementation strategies or are plausibly outweighed by the potential benefits of such modelling. They should be viewed as matters to be addressed in order to allow child protection workers the benefits of PRM, rather than as reasons to reject a potentially powerful element in an appropriate suite of child protection measures.

CHAPTER 6

Safeguarding Children Research
A United Kingdom Perspective

Trevor Spratt

Introduction

In developing a critique on safeguarding research in the UK over the early years of the new millennium, I am not seeking to provide a systematic review of all research undertaken in relation to safeguarding children. Essentially, this is because the great raft of research available is located across a number of professional domains, including neuroscience, psychology and medicine and is no longer the preserve (if indeed it ever was) of social work. Safeguarding research is now, and rightly so, reflective of new understandings of how the developing child interacts with multiple environments over time. Such understandings have had the effect of collapsing, in theory if not always in practice, professional silo walls in order to appreciate more fully the complex interactions between genetics and environments and track associations between childhood experiences across health and social circumstances over the life-course. In a sense the story of the new millennium is that research into the lives of children has become unbounded. Consequently, this chapter will seek to provide a critique of how ready social work may be to appreciate and use such research in the context of a political and policy environment wherein priorities are sensitive to public and media interpretations of which children should be prioritised for safeguarding.

Reflections on our base line:
attitudes and research capacity

In reflecting on the contribution of social work research to the safeguarding of children in the UK, my own view is that the case for professional knowledge being drawn in substantial part from research evidence should be central to practice. It is now well established that clinical judgement (or practice wisdom) is a less sure predicator of client outcomes than is assessment utilising actuarial instruments built upon research to establish statistical probability (Taylor 2010). This view, however, remains contested within social work, where suspicion of scientific method in some respects has had implications for the direction of safeguarding research, both hitherto and since the turn of the new millennium. The consequences may be detected in the quality and quantity of research.

By way of illustration, an analysis of the *British Journal of Social Work* paper by Hodge, Lacasse, and Benson (2012), titled 'Influential papers in social work discourse: The 100 most highly cited articles in disciplinary journals 2000–2009', reveals that the top three papers are concerned with the topic of evidence-based social work, with only 25 of the 100 papers (my estimate based on reviewing the titles) reporting empirical research. Social work as a profession appears more interested in ideas, as observed by Hodge *et al*.: 'A substantial proportion of the 100 most influential articles were conceptually or theoretically orientated' (p.77).

In addition to a propensity to theorise, research traditions in social work tend to favour qualitative methods. There are limited programmatic and systematic endeavours to test hypotheses. Part of the reason for this is the position of the subject within the academy, where the priority has often been to prepare the next generation of social workers for practice over development of an evidence base to support practice. This has resulted in a low research activity rate amongst social work academics.

The Research Assessment Exercises (RAE 2001 and 2008), UK-wide evaluations of research undertaken by academic institutions involving national and international peers and other relevant parties, provide some evidence for this assertion. It is not possible to disaggregate the measures for social work research within the 2008 RAE submissions as social work results were combined with social policy. With regard to quantity, Sharland (2009) observes that in the 2008 RAE out of an estimated 750 social work academics in the UK, 300 submissions were made with only some 75 producing research outputs of an empirical nature. Results from a comparable national exercise (Research Excellence Framework, REF 2014) found an increase in large-scale multi-method empirical studies in social work.[1]

In relation to quality, Marsh and colleagues (2005) note that 43 per cent of the work submitted by social work in the 2001 RAE was rated of national or international excellence, which compared unfavourably to departments of General Practice (88%). Shaw and Norton (2008) cite a RAE 2001 figure of 24.3 per cent of submissions concerned with research in the area of children, young people and their families. So, if the research outputs submitted total approximately 1200 (this is an inflated estimate as not all submissions will reach the four per individual level), those concerning children and families total approximately 300 (assuming the 2001 proportion remains similar in 2008) in number, with an estimated 30 reporting empirical research.

This is not a measure of all research undertaken in the UK, as not all research publications will have been submitted. Furthermore, it is not known if child and family research is under- (or indeed over-) represented in the empirical category, partly due to the integrated nature of RAE 2008. Nevertheless, it serves as the nearest measure of the quantity and quality of social work research in the UK. So, when talking about social work research in relation to child safeguarding, there is not very much, and little of an empirical nature. This general observation on the landscape does not give full recognition to those examples (although perhaps few in number) of programmatic research, for example, studies carried out in response to the UK Government's Safeguarding Children Research Initiative (discussed later).[2]

The shifting political and policy contexts

Whilst stimuli such as the Safeguarding Children Research Initiative (above) are welcome, it is important to pay due regard to the political and policy contexts. Research does not take place, nor are its products put to work, in a political vacuum. The reach of politics into the everyday world of social work has implications for what research gets done and what research gets used, this being particularly evident in England.

Reflecting on what constitutes safeguarding is, at least in part, shaped by the fluid interpretations of politicians. Nigel Parton (2011)

---

1   See: www.ref.ac.uk/panels/paneloverviewreports/, (p.87).

2   www.gov.uk/government/publications/safeguarding-children-across-services-messages-from-research.

observes that the idea of safeguarding under New Labour (the Labour Government elected in 1997) represented an attempt to further widen the number of children for whom the state should play a part in ensuring that their welfare was both safeguarded and promoted. This extension included children in need of protection from abuse and neglect and those who could benefit from a range of services progressively targeted towards meeting increasing levels of need. The Every Child Matters policy (Department for Education and Skills 2004) was to mark the highpoint of this progressive and inclusive view in relation to the state's role in optimising the development of the nation's children. State interventions were regarded as founded on a solid evidential base, as UK Prime Minister (1997–2007) Tony Blair's speech to the Rowntree Foundation (a charity for social justice) in 2006 illustrates:

> Where it is clear, as it very often is, at a young age, that children are at risk of being brought up in a dysfunctional home where there are multiple problems, say of drug abuse or offending, then instead of waiting [...] we should act early enough, with the right help, support and disciplined frame-work for the family to prevent it [...] You can detect and predict the children and families likely to go wrong. (Blair 2006)

The concern was to use findings from epidemiological studies (distribution of health and illness in populations) to locate the most vulnerable children, based on calculation as to the future probability of poor outcomes on the analysis of current circumstances. Such calculations were not based on identification of single incidents of abuse within families, but rather on a count of adversities: the higher the number, the greater the increase in probability of poor future outcomes.

A subsequent retrenchment to a narrower concentration on those children at most immediate risk of abuse and neglect followed the death of a 17-month-old child Peter Connolly, in 2006, despite repeated contact with social and health services and the election of a Conservative/Liberal Democrat Coalition Government in the UK in 2010. A Minister for Education (2010–2014), Michael Gove, focused on those most vulnerable children for whom early and permanent removal to care, in situations where parents were unable to provide acceptable levels of care, was both necessary and supported by research. In a speech to the Institute of Public Policy Research (an independent think tank) in 2012 he stated:

When Professor Elaine Farmer (a social work academic) and colleagues carried out a five-year follow up study of neglected children returned home, they found that even when we do intervene we still return children to abusive homes too early – and in too many cases. She studied 138 neglected children who had been returned to their families. After two years, 59 per cent of children returned home had been abused or neglected, and after five years, 65 per cent of returns home had ended. (Gove 2012)

Later in the same speech Gove drew attention to counterarguments regarding risks inherent within the public care system:

Those who point to the numbers in prison, or suffering mental health problems, or in poor schools, or without qualifications, or who are unemployed and who are, or have been in care, and conclude that it is always care that is responsible for these terrible outcomes, are making a terrible error. They are confusing correlation and causation.

Quite, but not perhaps grounds for dismissal as 'terrible errors'. The point here is that the selective use of research to highlight the outcomes of placement decisions over relatively short timescales (five years being just about a term of a government) demonstrates renewed preoccupations with those children who are most visibly vulnerable, and subject to child protection interventions. Prioritising the safeguarding of the few rather than the many.

This selective use of research occurs in a climate where public censure of professional practices following inquiries into the death or serious harm of children from abuse and neglect heavily influences political debate in the UK. In the wake of inquiries, oscillations arise between basing interventions on research-informed preventative programmatic interventions based on prediction and applied to a broader population and those individually targeted in response to abuse or neglect. Such swings create uncertainty as to who requires safeguarding and in what way: the designated group of 'Children in Need' under the Children Act 1989 (England and Wales), where services are intended to enhance developmental outcomes where difficulties are present; or a narrower group of children who require child protection services to prevent abuse and, or neglect? In legislation this is not a matter of either/or, but in policy and practice it often is.

The two narratives of child safeguarding research: public health and child protection

The political uses of research illustrate different narratives at play in safeguarding research, reflecting two conceptualisations of child safeguarding. The first of these is a *public health narrative* (Scott 2006). This is concerned with identifying populations of children at most risk of poor outcomes (including abuse), at the earliest possible stage, on the basis of assessment of risk factors to inform evidence-based interventions (Sheldon and Macdonald 2009). This narrative promotes research across a number of fields, including neuroscience, psychology and physical and mental health, to study sub-optimal childhood environments in order to measure physiological, psychological and social effects on development across the life-course. Advances in understanding genetic and environmental interactions are informing a new model of child development (Center on the Developing Child at Harvard University 2010). Ecological theory is becoming the normative way for professions, including social work, to conceptualise the impact upon children of multiple and interconnected developmental influences, some proximal (or downstream), some distal (or upstream) and some longitudinal.

The unintended effect of suggested interconnectivity has, however, been to threaten professional shibboleths. In some cases this has led to intellectual *land grabs*. For example, in the light of research demonstrating associations between adverse childhood experiences and later onset of disease in middle age (Anda *et al.* 2010), the American Pediatric Society argue that such diseases are essentially late manifestations of the developmental problems of childhood (Shonkoff and Garner 2012). The research orientation is more often provided by international organisations such as the World Health Organization, which, in its report *Prevention of Child Maltreatment*, treats the experience of adversities in childhood as a public health concern, impacting on health across the life-course (Butchart *et al.* 2006). It is interesting to note that the behaviours that link experience of childhood adversities with later health outcomes are often via self-medicating pathways – short-term stress ameliorative behaviours, such as smoking, that relieve psychological stress but create physiological problems. Whilst such research will be familiar to social work academics, they are not much involved in its production. This is evident in the landmark series on child maltreatment research published in the *Lancet* in 2009 (Gilbert *et al.* 2009), authored in the main by medical scientists, albeit with some representation from social work researchers.

The second narrative is *child protection*. It is concerned with identifying those children who have suffered or are likely to suffer abuse, their progress through child protection systems and their outcomes. Such outcomes largely concentrate on short-term concern for the safety of children in the community, with a wider and longer-term set of outcomes concentrated on children in state care. This is the more familiar territory of social work research, reflecting a concern to study what we do and how we do it, and track the consequences.

Whilst the child protection narrative pays due homage to the place of research evidence (Ward *et al.* 2010), the dominant points of reference have traditionally been guidance published by successive governments, often forged in the aftermath of child death inquiries and, more latterly, the findings of Case Management Reviews (English multidisciplinary reviews of cases of serious injury or death when child abuse or neglect is suspected or known) (Brandon *et al.* 2008). Dominant concerns have been to examine child and familial characteristics (types of families) and patterns of professional communication and intervention to detect recurring patterns.

Such concerns are reflected in the research commissioning patterns of government: the Department of Education's (DfE) *Safeguarding Children Across Services: Messages from Research on Identifying and Responding to Child Maltreatment* (Davies and Ward 2011) reporting research commissioned as part of the Government's response to the *The Victoria Climbié Inquiry: Report of an Inquiry by Lord Laming* (Laming 2003). The purpose of the commissioned research was to provide a stronger evidence base to improve three areas identified as critical. These are: 'identification and initial response to abuse and neglect', 'effective interventions after abuse or its likelihood have been identified' and 'effective interagency and interdisciplinary working'. Whilst the aims concentrate on the most vulnerable of children, the reported research findings suggest a narrowing of the gap between public health and child protection narratives.

Public health and child protection narratives: how do they 'play out' in practice?

The DfE's report (Davies and Ward 2011) provides a bridge between the two narratives, drawing our attention to the fact that *both* probability of abuse *and* poor long-term outcomes (social, emotional, physical and mental health), are increased when children are living in situations where parents are suffering poor mental health, misusing drugs and or alcohol and caught up in domestic violence, often experienced in the context of financial and housing problems with inadequate familial and neighbourhood supports. An influential compilation of government-sponsored research from an earlier time, *Child Protection: Messages from Research* (Department of Health 1995), directed the attention of professionals to the plight of children living in low-warmth/high-criticism environments. The report also draws attention to emotional abuse and neglect experienced in early childhood and adolescent periods, citing the wider body of research on child development, which shows these two periods to be crucial in their influence upon future outcomes across the life-course.

Drawing on the work of Daniel, Taylor and Scott (2009a), the DfE report (Davies and Ward 2011) observes that: 'Neglect and emotional abuse only rarely result in crises, so practitioners need to look for evidence of long term, chronic maltreatment' (2011, p.5). The developmental link between the two reports is that an observed phenomenon has become a research-informed phenomenon, directing our attention to the need to move beyond (metaphorically) suppuration points to act earlier and effectively in children's lives.

The message that early interventions are critical to forestall or to ameliorate damage to the developing child is now central to the safeguarding debate (Allen 2011). The DfE report emphasises that 'a wide variety of universal and population approaches are available at both primary (aimed at whole populations) and secondary (targeted at vulnerable or 'at risk' populations) levels to prevent the occurrence of abuse and neglect' (Davies and Ward 2011, p.7). Whilst research demonstrates outcomes for children have improved where social work is built upon careful assessment and robust case management, it tends to be those families who are subject to child protection processes (i.e. investigation), case conference and child protection planning, who receive such interventions (Farmer and Lutman 2009). This finding echoes another *Child Protection: Messages from Research* (Department of Health 1995) theme that children have to be designated as in need of protection to access services and, as a consequence, services to the wider population of 'Children in Need' remain underdeveloped.

My own research with colleagues has largely concentrated on two interrelated areas: first, how well placed are local authorities in the UK to identify, at the earliest possible points, those children and their families whose characteristics indicate increased probability of poor outcomes, including but not restricted to, the experience of abuse

(Hayes and Spratt 2009; Spratt 2001, 2014)? And second, to develop new perspectives to assist local authorities in utilising research from other fields to reconceptualise the referred population, identifying within it those children, on the basis of probability, who are most likely to experience poor outcomes (Spratt 2012).

Our examination of the child welfare system in Northern Ireland demonstrated that considerable differences existed between practitioners and managers in the interpretation of threshold criteria, namely demarcating a boundary between those children requiring immediate protection and child welfare cases requiring a broader family support response. However, most child welfare cases were found to feature concerns over parental care/behaviour and consequently the system featured a two-tier response, one termed *child protection* and the other *child protection light*, the second largely mirroring the processes of the first. The emphasis in both types of responses was on managing risk, featuring multidisciplinary contact, assessment and, in most cases, quick closure, with only a small minority of families being offered services. If the majority of referrals receive in essence a form of child protection response focused on managing risks, then reported reductions in official child protection statistics may not be indicative of a shift in practice to a more accessible, family-engaging and needs-led approach as suggested in policy.

Judgements by social workers are not solely based on a detached evaluation of risk to the child, but also take account of the risks pertaining to themselves if they are later judged to have made predictive 'errors' concerning a child's safety. This may help to explain oscillations in system output measures, for example the rise by almost 50 per cent in care applications to the English courts in the second half of 2008–09 following the death of Peter Connolly (discussed earlier) (Parton 2011). That the system for safeguarding children should default to risk-averse behaviour is perfectly understandable in the light of public intolerance to tragic individual case outcomes. My own work with colleagues has sought to demonstrate the utility of using risk assessment tools to help inform professional decisions (Spratt 2012). Whilst the predictive power of such instruments has been demonstrated to consistently outweigh professional judgement (Shlonsky and Wagner 2005), there have been considerable difficulties in using them in practice. These include lack of training in statistical interpretation and a perception that individual 'cases are much harder to assess using a rationalist risk paradigm of prediction and control' (Broadhurst *et al.* 2010, p.1050). This is unfortunate as instruments can be adapted to inform professional judgement to enhance predictive accuracy, assist case prioritisation and offer an evidence-based defence in how risk is calculated and used to inform interventions. Our particular project has been to undertake research to help practitioners to identify those cases where childhood experiences of multiple adversities increases probability of experiencing poor outcomes, including abuse, across the life-course (Davidson, Devaney and Spratt 2010; McGavock and Spratt 2014).

One example of how such research may inform identification and prioritisation are cases where domestic violence is the reason for referral. Research by Stanley and colleagues (2010) indicates that 83 per cent (n=251) of cases referred for reasons of children witnessing domestic violence received either a follow-up letter or no further action from local authority social workers. Those who received a social work visit did so because the family was previously known to social workers or the child had been caught up in the violence. However, research by McGavock (2012) demonstrates that witnessing domestic violence is a key indicator for the presence of additional childhood adversities, including abuse and neglect.

Whilst safeguarding children at the point of referral may be slow to utilise research evidence, there are encouraging examples of projects that embed research in practice. The Family Intervention Projects (FIPs) represent a targeted response to families where assessment suggests multiple problems (Lexmond, Bazalgette and Margo 2011). The project involves contract-based multidisciplinary intensive interventions. In a literature review to support the development of good practice with families with complex needs, Lea (2011) identified that:

> The majority of families [...] were identified through existing contact with services. Identification of families can be viewed as threefold; through existing contact with services, identification through disparate datasets to identify those at risk of developing complex needs and identification of areas that may contain higher concentrations of families with complex needs. (pp.77–78)

Initiatives such as FIPs span public health and child protection narratives, recognising the need to engage effectively with those already known to services, whilst seeking to use data and area indicators to identify families with similar characteristics and needs.

Building on what we already know

Whilst providing examples of the effectiveness of research informing practice in a linear fashion may be problematic, there is another way of understanding the contribution of research to safeguarding children. We might term this 'the influence of research by gradual absorption'.

The way we think about active and passive smoking today is informed by public health campaigns. Whilst we are unlikely to have much knowledge of the foundational work of Sir Richard Doll in establishing the link between tobacco smoking and lung disease (Doll and Hill 1950), the now culturally embedded view that smoking is linked to poor health is built upon his work. In similar ways we now come to think of physical, sexual and emotional abuse and neglect as bad for children, not only because such phenomena are unacceptable to contemporary values and deny the rights of children (although both these factors are of influence). How do we know? Because for over half a century we have been researching the associations between the experiences of abuse and neglect and later outcomes (Davidson *et al.* 2010). And such awareness is not without effect.

Radford and colleagues (2011) interviewed a national (UK) representative sample of children and young people to examine trends in child abuse and neglect. They suggest a continuing significant presence of both but in comparison with a similar, earlier study (1998), argue 'that many childhoods have changed for the better over the last 30 years. Overall, the young adults in 2009 reported less physical, sexual and verbal abuse during their childhoods than those interviewed previously' (p.4). In considering possible reasons for the reduction in some forms of abuse, the authors note that 'it is difficult to weigh the state's contribution to reducing child abuse and neglect against the actions taken by individuals and communities through long-term social change' (p.5). They also observed that the numbers of children of all ages on a child protection plan or register is far lower than the estimated number of children experiencing maltreatment.

Whilst actions taken by individuals and communities *and* professionals, may be influenced by research absorbed gradually, it is nevertheless important to identify the specific contribution of professional practice as indicated by research. Devaney's (2009) work demonstrates that social workers are effective in keeping those children who are subjects of child protection plans safe from the experience of repeated abuse. And, in relation to those most serious of cases where there are concerns for a child's life, Pritchard and Williams (2010), in their examination of falling child mortality rates, attribute part of this reduction to professional intervention and note: '[A]s the media readily blame social work for the high-profile tragedies [...] they may begin to acknowledge something of social work's probable contribution to the achievements over the past thirty years' (p.1715). Reasons perhaps for cautious optimism?

Challenges ahead

Social work has made safeguarding children in the short term, where dangers are evident, an area of expertise, a reflexive default sustained by risk-averse politics and practices, sensitive to public opinion. This child protection narrative may sit uneasily with a public health narrative, which aids identification of a wider population of children whose characteristics are predictive of poor outcomes over the life-course.

Are there ways to build bridges between child protection and public health narratives in safeguarding research? I believe there are three starting points for such an endeavour: first is to examine the place that research evidence should play in practice; second, to consider how to increase research capacity in social work; third, to seek to bring the unique perspective of social work to research on safeguarding children through joint projects working together with colleagues from other disciplines. The unbounded nature of research into the lives of children provides an unprecedented opportunity for social work to inform and utilise safeguarding research.

CHAPTER 7

Research in Child Abuse and Neglect
A Finnish Perspective

Tarja Pösö

Introduction

There is a distinctive conceptual puzzle in how to address research in child abuse and neglect in the Finnish context. This is because the national research communities do not conventionally use the concept of child abuse and neglect. Instead, researchers in health- and nursing-related studies tend to use the term 'child maltreatment'; and in studies related to social research, 'family/domestic violence' or 'children exposed to violence' are the terms generally used. In social work research, the terminology is currently even more diffuse.

Previously, the concept of abuse and neglect belonged to child welfare policy and practice in the period from the early 20th century until the early 1980s, which encompassed the first Child Welfare Act (Lastensuojelulaki 52/1936). When this original Act was replaced in 1983 (Lastensuojelulaki 683/1983), the concept of abuse and neglect disappeared from the legislation. The main task of child welfare was redefined to provide services to families and children in need and at risk instead of only protecting children from abuse and neglect. Since then, the concepts of child abuse and neglect have not been part of the core social work terminology. The Finnish child welfare system, described in a cross-country comparative analysis as a family-service model with child centric orientation (Pösö 2011), addresses its most common issues in practice as being 'use of in-home services', 'parental substance abuse and mental health problems', 'problems in parenting' and 'child's own behaviour', thus excluding the notion of violence of any kind.

The other major change in legislation regarding children also took place in the early 1980s when the ban against corporal punishment was introduced by the Child Custody and Right of Access Act (Laki lapsen huollosta ja tapaamisoikeudesta 361/1983). Since 1983, the use of violence of any kind has been forbidden in relations between children and parents. This ban could suggest that child abuse had disappeared from Finnish childhood and therefore eliminated the need for a corresponding conceptual clarity and rigour in research, policy and practice. However, when the first Child Victim Survey was carried out in 2008, the everyday nature of violence in children's lives was vividly demonstrated, highlighting new forms of violence, for example web-based violence, that threaten children as well (Ellonen *et al.* 2008). In addition, there are messages about the growth in social inequalities, leading to families and children experiencing poverty, the threat of poverty and other forms of social exclusion (Bardy and Heino 2013).

Conceptually, child abuse and neglect are understood in this chapter as active and passive, direct and indirect forms of violence targeted at children. The focus is on the family setting in particular but some explorations of violence in other childhood environments are carried out as well. The terms 'children exposed to violence' and 'violence towards children' will be used to highlight the position and rights of children in violence (Eriksson 2012). Instead of being a systematic review of all Finnish research looking at 'child abuse and neglect', the chapter aims to be a critical reading of the existing studies and their core messages for policy and practice to safeguard children. The reading is done from the point of view of a child welfare/social work researcher. This is not only a personal choice, but a choice that is argued for by the fact that child welfare services have long been criticised for being insensitive towards issues of violence (Hiitola 2011; Pösö 1997). Likewise, special attention will be given to those issues, which have been ignored in Finnish research.

Mapping out the landscape of research

Although the body of research on child abuse and neglect is not expansive and does not make a distinctive field of study in Finland, three major thematic areas may be found: first, research on professionals and authorities; second, on self-reported violence; and third on symptoms and social structures related to violence. All three will be described in more detail in the following sections. Most of the studies have been published only in Finnish; if some English language publications are known to exist, they are used in this article.

Focusing on professionals and authorities

In contrast with the previous decades, since 2010 there have been two public inquiries into violence experienced by children. The first was carried out as a result of the sudden increase in the number of children and spouses dying due to domestic violence (familicide, filicide) (Ministry of the Interior 2012). This was based on the records of the authorities (including police, health care and social welfare) of all children below the age of 15 who had died between 2003 and 2012 due to familicide, neonaticide or other forms of violence by the parent; however, 2011 was exceptional with 13 deaths. The inquiry argues that all the deaths shared certain similar factors, such as problems in the relations between spouses and crises related to divorce as well as parents' problems with substance abuse and mental health. The second examined the violent death of a girl who was known to child welfare services (Ministry of Justice 2013). Although the inquiries were not technically research, they are noteworthy because such public inquiries or serious case reviews are not common practice in Finland. Both inquiries recommended a number of fundamental changes in early interventions and interagency and inter-professional services as well as in the exchange of information among authorities.

These inquiries, together with national policy programmes on children and child safety (e.g. Ministry of the Interior 2008), demonstrate that there is a new interest in how service systems and professionals meet children. This interest is not, however, reflected in research: very little research is directed at what the authorities actually do with children exposed to violence and how they view their own role. In this respect, there is a mismatch between the key policy landmarks and existing research knowledge. Nevertheless, studies on professionals and authorities form a recognisable part of child abuse and neglect research.

The study by Humppi and Ellonen (2010), focusing on the interagency reporting practices of authorities, uniquely covers a wide array of authorities. They conducted 33 interviews with police officers, social workers, doctors, and school and day care personnel in three Finnish municipalities; all the interviewees had been involved at least once in reporting a suspicion of violence against children, leading to a police investigation. Documentary data was also analysed: this consisted of 216 cases of violence against children reported to and investigated by police in the same three municipalities in the same year. The study highlights several gaps in the reporting practices of the authorities: the authorities were aware of their mandatory duty to report but did not fulfil it. These gaps have later been called 'hesitation' (Ellonen and Pösö 2014). 'Hesitation' means that authorities employ certain practices on whether to act or not to act, and the boundary between the different responses is negotiated on a case-by-case basis. Agency-based rules play an important role: clear agency-based rules and cultures support practitioners to overcome hesitation. Yet, the very existence of hesitation demonstrates that the legislative norms of mandatory reporting and interagency reporting are not systematically followed (Ellonen and Pösö 2014; Humppi and Ellonen 2010). Studies looking at the recognition of domestic violence as part of health care support (e.g. Husso *et al.* 2012) and family guidance (e.g. Keskinen 2005) support the view on hesitation as a characteristic of professional practice.

Child welfare practice has been studied by Hiitola (2011) through analysis of social workers' case files and written decisions of the administrative courts in care order decision-making. The corpus of her data consists of all court cases (343) in the administrative courts in 2008. Her interest was in exploring how forms of (domestic) violence are represented in case files and written decisions. The results highlight the brevity and even absence of descriptions of alleged violence. The victim and/or the perpetrator were mentioned only in passing. Four different discourses for presenting and explaining violence were found: conflicts between parents, the mother's failure to protect the child, problems with substance abuse and violence, and disciplinary violence. What is notable here is that in this particular analysis there was no specific discourse to address the abuse from the child's point of view. Hiitola's conclusion is that child welfare practice is not sensitive towards the issues of violence.

The paragraphs above highlight one mainstream agenda of knowledge production in Finland regarding children exposed to violence: focusing on recognising and reporting violence, as informed by practitioners in interviews or relevant case files. A similar focus on recognising and reporting is found in the systematic research review by Paavilainen and Flinck (2014) examining international studies published in English language journals. Practices *with* children exposed to violence have only been occasionally studied (e.g. Eskonen 2005; Forsberg 2005), leaving a considerable gap in research-based knowledge about the authorities and professionals meeting child abuse and neglect. Professionals identify and report violence, liaise with other colleagues and work with children to protect them from further harm and to help them cope with their abusive experiences. Very little is known about these practices, their dynamics and outcomes.

Asking children and parents

The second mainstream – though new – agenda of research on children exposed to violence is based on self-report studies. Instead of examining violence as known by professionals and authorities, researchers have asked children (and parents) how often and what kind of violence they experience in their everyday life. The first Finnish Child Victim Survey was conducted in 2008 (Ellonen *et al.* 2008). Previously, a smaller survey had been carried out about children's experience of violence in the home (Sariola 1990). In the more recent study, the two groups of research informants were 12–13-year-olds and 15–16-year-olds. They answered a web-based questionnaire at schools during the school day. The data was a representative sample of mainland Finland and its Finnish- and Swedish-speaking children within these two age groups: the final sample consisted of 13,459 respondents. The study highlighted the everyday nature of violent experiences among children and young people (Ellonen *et al.* 2008). Home and other everyday environments included violent incidents. The researchers compared the child survey results with adult crime victimisation survey results. Although the survey results are not entirely comparable, they suggest that children are exposed to considerably higher levels of violence than adults (Ellonen *et al.* 2008).

In addition, the Child Victim Survey highlights that a significant number of children's experiences of violence are related to domestic violence: they either witness violence among their parents and other family members or they also experience direct violence targeted towards them. Yet, the study claims that there has been a clear reduction in corporal punishment and other forms of parental violence since the earlier survey (Sariola 1990) over 20 years ago (Ellonen *et al.* 2008). A surprising finding of the survey is that children living with their parents at home experience more physically violent acts by adults than children living in residential care institutions or foster homes (Ellonen and Pösö 2011). The sample included a similar proportion of children in out-of-home care to that in the National Child Welfare statistics, making this comparison relevant. This is a hypothetical finding due to several conceptual and methodological challenges related to violence; however, it does still highlight home as being a distinctively common place for violence against children.

After the 2008 Child Victim Survey, a separate survey of parents was conducted in 2011 to learn about their abusive behaviour towards their children aged 0–12 as part of solving conflicts within the family (Ellonen 2012). More than 3000 parents, mainly mothers, joined the survey. Although the survey was about a topic considered sensitive – and culturally even taboo – parents responded to it as actively as Finnish people answer postal surveys in general (response rate 53%). The survey results highlight that parents have negative attitudes towards corporal punishment and that they are aware of the formal legislation against the parental use of violence. This understanding was also reflected in reports of their own behaviour: most of them did not report any violent behaviour towards their children. Less than 1 per cent of the mothers and fathers reported that they had used the most serious forms of violence, such as punching, kicking or hitting a child with an object. A further analysis demonstrated that parents using serious forms of violence had experienced corporal punishment themselves in their childhood. The reporting of the use of severe violence was most common in families with several children; families reporting severe forms of violence and those reporting no violence did not otherwise differ in terms of education or social standing. In addition, the mothers reporting the use of severe forms of violence were those who felt that they had not received any adequate help from the welfare services despite having called for help (Ellonen 2012).

The studies mentioned above demonstrate the interest in learning about the victim experiences of children or the abusive behaviour of parents by asking children and parents themselves. The survey format has been much used, suggesting that other methods of inquiry have only been occasionally used and mainly related to young people rather than children (e.g. Honkatukia, Nyqvist and Pösö 2006) or to adults to learn about their childhood experiences of abuse (e.g. Hurtig 2013; Laitinen 2004). The strong focus on the survey tool is noteworthy, as studies on domestic violence, especially analysing spousal violence, have employed a wider choice of methods, including interviews, ethnography and other qualitative approaches (e.g. Keskinen 2005).

In contrast to some countries with strict regulations and lack of research access to children or data concerning their experiences of violence (e.g. Hayes and Devaney 2004), the regulation of research ethics in Finland are such that they should not directly explain the limited and fragmentary nature of research knowledge about children exposed to violence. There is little in-depth analysis of how ethically sound research could be carried out in this particular field of study. Indeed, how to balance children's entitlement to a voice and the right not to be abused again by the research itself is a challenge: research can in many ways be used to silence children and marginalise their experiences (Cater and Överlien 2014; Mudaly and Goddard 2006). Children who completed the Child Victim Survey were asked how they felt about the survey, and an interesting result was found: those children who had experienced violence reported positive views about the survey more often than those children who had not had any experiences of violence (Ellonen and Pösö 2011). This finding poses an important dilemma about the use of such survey-based general studies: should one prioritise the knowledge that children without any experiences of violence found the survey somewhat inconvenient over the knowledge that children with violence experiences found it important that someone asked about their experience?

Studies focusing on symptoms and social inequality

In addition to studying violence as an issue for professionals or as an experience by children, there is a recognisable interest in studying the symptoms of violence and social structures that may enable violence. This interest includes indirect violence and neglect and encompasses a somewhat diffuse field of study. Studies of children with foetal alcohol spectrum disorders provide a good example of research focusing on symptoms (e.g. Koponen *et al.* 2013). This strand of research is salient to the vivid and contradictory Finnish policy and debates on whether pregnant women who are heavy users of alcohol and drugs should be treated against their will or whether policy should rest more on developing services on a voluntary basis. Trauma-focused studies, carried out mainly by scholars of psychology and medicine, could be seen as other examples of symptom-focused studies on children exposed to violence (e.g. Peltonen 2011).

Studies on the effects of social inequalities are not conventionally seen as related to child abuse and violence, although issues of poverty, exclusion from education and labour market and intergenerational inheritance of social problems (e.g. Hämäläinen and Kangas 2010; Kataja *et al.* 2014) are considered relevant for studying neglect. This branch of research tends to use national administrative and statistical registers of people and their participation in labour marker or education for their data and casts light on the macro-level dynamics of social inequalities. The most alarming recent message has been the growth in child poverty and families with children living in poverty, although numbers are still low in the European context (Jäntti 2010). In his study, using relevant register data, Heikki Hiilamo (2009) analysed the number of out-of-home placements in relation to general socioeconomic indicators and other so-called risk factors in the period between 1991 and 2007 on the national level. The study shows clearly that the growth in out-of-home placements is associated with an increase in long-term economic hardships, as well as parental/caregiver alcohol and substance abuse. However, messages from research on social inequalities are not always translated to 'child neglect', social inequalities being treated as social and historical contexts (e.g. Bardy and Heino 2013). The reason for this may lie in the fact that social inequalities are studied on the macro level, whereas neglect is seen more as a micro-level issue of individuals, families and communities.

Shortcomings of the research

In sum, the landscape of studies on children exposed to violence includes certain thematic highlights as demonstrated above. The body of research is expanding and it is reflected in the number of publications within the last ten years or so. Yet the present landscape of research and research-based knowledge is still rather diverse and thematically fragmented. Three major shortcomings are evident.

First, very little is known about the relations of violence experienced by children and professional practices within welfare organisations. The focus has been on identifying and reporting violence. It would be especially important to have a more nuanced understanding of how children exposed to violence are met by services and practitioners, and how services meet children's needs, rights and agency. One such question, for example, is how the position of children in relation to their parents or other carer is negotiated in cases of domestic violence. There are some hints in research suggesting that the importance of keeping up family ties, which is strongly emphasised by the present child welfare policy and practice, may be used to justify overcoming children's reluctance to be in touch with an abusive parent (e.g. Forsberg and Pösö 2008). Indeed, parents'/adults' rights to their children may sometimes overshadow children's rights to a non-abusive everyday life (Forsberg and Pösö 2008; Hurtig 2013) despite the negative attitude towards violence in Finnish society.

The second thematic shortcoming of the present research, closely related to the previous one, is that very little is known about the actual outcome of interventions against violence. There is a lack of empirical studies; most importantly, there is also a lack of theoretical and ideological analysis of what could and should be seen as a good outcome of such interventions.

Third, very little is known about neglect. Although notions of 'poor parenting' and 'lack of appropriate parental skills' are common terminology in child welfare, very few systematic empirical or theoretical explorations have been carried out. Neglect is interrelated with the social and cultural norms of what is seen as appropriate upbringing and care. Thus, critical social analysis would be needed to examine the role and dynamics of cultural and social norms that are set for appropriate family relations.

Messages from research to practice and policy

Corporal punishment and bullying at school make excellent examples of how policy and practice have taken some forms of violence into consideration. Corporal punishment was forbidden by law in 1983, and bullying is now a focus of nationwide programmes at schools (e.g. Salmivalli and Poskiparta 2012). Forensic investigation teams have been established in certain health care units and the concept of a 'children's house', a specialised multi-professional service examining and helping with the investigation of children exposed to (sexual) violence, will be introduced in the near future in Finland. The role and position of research-based knowledge varies in these undertakings. The school anti-bullying programme is a research-intense programme in which research knowledge has guided the programme; and, vice versa, the programme has been studied and evaluated by research. Yet the interconnections between research, policy and practice in general are far from strong.

In particular, the statutory tasks of child welfare services regarding violence towards children have only been weakly developed, analysed or evaluated based on research knowledge. Child welfare services are, however, the key institutions to meet serious and complex forms of violence. They are interconnected with many other welfare services and the police. The role of the latter has changed during recent years as the legislative norms about the social workers' duty to notify the police have increased. Thus it would be topical to examine what kind of knowledge of violence child welfare services are based on and how the related interventions function.

The Finnish system is different from many child welfare systems known in the Anglo-American countries in that it aims to provide services, mainly of a voluntary nature, to children and families to support their welfare. The threshold for services is not based on experiences of direct or indirect violence (abuse or neglect) alone, but 'the need' for child welfare services based on the likelihood of risks of different kinds for the child's health and development. Therefore, a variety of childhood and family problems are met by the services. This forms the context in which social workers identify, report and work with children exposed to violence. Consequently, the children's experiences of violence may be overlooked or they may become conceptualised differently (e.g. mother's tiredness, Hiitola 2011; Pösö 1997).

The strengths and weaknesses of this system emphasising such a holistic approach have not been analysed or examined in detail. This is very topical as there are contradictory views on how the Finnish child welfare system should be changed. There is a growing body of concern that the system ignores even serious forms of violence and that a more carefully violence-focused investigative system and interagency practices are needed (e.g. Ministry of Justice 2013). Alternatively, recent policy reports suggest that the welfare focus should be developed to meet service users' needs more holistically and personally (e.g. Ministry of Social Affairs and Health 2013). It is likely, however, that decisions on any direction of system change will be more informed by policy preferences than by careful and comprehensive research analysis. Not to study violence is an active choice and should be ethically argued by the research communities (Paavilainen, Lepistö and Flinck 2014).

Conclusion

The critical message from this review of Finnish literature is the fragmentary body of research knowledge about child abuse and neglect and the interventions dealing with those experiences. It is noteworthy that this particular issue – how to help children to cope with the experiences of violence when the family relations as such are abusive – has been overshadowed by studying the prevalence of different forms of violence and by the policy attempts to identify and report violence more intensely. The particular weak point is the statutory child welfare services, as the research that informs child welfare practice and policy about the successful forms of services and interventions for children exposed to violence, and analyses the outcomes of those interventions, is almost non-existent.

The conceptual vagueness mentioned at the beginning of this chapter thus gives a significant message about the Finnish research in this area. Although violence has been studied from certain perspectives and fundamental legal and social responses have been introduced against violence, the very violence in the child welfare context, as a topic for study and practice, has been somewhat ignored. Following Øverlien's (2010) calls for further research, based on a thorough review of international literature published in English, one could say that in Finland there is a particular need to learn more longitudinally, both quantitatively and qualitatively, how child abuse and neglect are understood and met by child welfare practitioners; how the responses are chosen and what kind of implications they have for different parties, including the children, parents and practitioners; and how different parties act and make sense of these responses. Consequently, a critical evaluation of the conceptual vagueness to address 'child abuse and neglect' should be revisited and analysed in relation to the holistic approach of the Finnish attempts to safeguard children.

CHAPTER 8

Research in Child Protection

An Australian Perspective

Fiona Arney, Leah Bromfield and Stewart McDougall

Introduction

The statistics describing abuse and neglect of Australian children are confronting. Approximately 1 in 10 Australian adults have experienced physical abuse in childhood, and 1 in 20 boys and 1 in 10 girls have experienced penetrative sexual abuse (Price-Robertson, Bromfield and Vassallo 2010). At any one time there are more than 40,000 children in state care across Australia (Productivity Commission 2014). Indigenous children are almost ten times as likely as non-Indigenous children to enter state care, and in South Australia it has been estimated that more than half of the Aboriginal children born in 2002 were the subject of a notification to the child protection system by the time they were four years old (Delfabbro *et al.* 2010a). Despite these figures, child protection research has only been a specialism in Australia in recent years as formal state systems of intervention have grown in size and scope. This comes in part in response to the numerous inquiries (e.g. Carmody 2013; Northern Territory Government 2010), which have found that state and territory systems of child protection are costly and inefficient, while the evidence base for alternatives remains sparse.

Compared with other social problems there has been little research to inform policy makers and service providers on the most effective strategies to prevent and respond to child abuse and neglect. To provide information to halt the escalating number of reports of child maltreatment, the Australian federal, state and territory governments, and non-government organisations have made various investments in child protection research and its dissemination.

In the mid-to-late 2000s, significant research concentrations with a focus on child protection and vulnerable families were established nationally (the Australian Centre for Child Protection) and in a number of states and territories across Australia (e.g. the Institute for Child Protection Studies in the Australian Capital Territory, the Child Protection Research Program in the Northern Territory, the Alfred Felton Chair in Child Welfare in Victoria, the Life without Barriers Carol Peltola Chair in Queensland, the Centre for Parenting Research in New South Wales). The aims of these organisations have been twofold: first to build the evidence base through applied primary and trans-disciplinary research, secondary data analysis, literature review and synthesis; and second, to enhance Australian research capacity via research training schemes (e.g. Honours and PhD programmes) and close relationships with government and non-government funders to translate research findings into practice and policy. The Australian National Child Protection Clearinghouse at the Australian Institute of Family Studies, and its successor, the Child Family Community Australia (CFCA) Research Policy and Practice Information Exchange,[1] along with the Children of Parents with a Mental Illness (COPMI) initiative,[2] were developed to facilitate this translation at a national level.

Taking stock of Australian child protection research

While there has been a considerable increase in child protection research activity in Australia since 2000, there are still many gaps in the knowledge base making it difficult to truly advance policy that is either based on or at the very least informed by research evidence (Mildon and Shlonsky 2011). In part, some of these gaps exist because of the fragmented nature of the Australian child welfare system. Protecting vulnerable children is traditionally seen as the responsibility of child protection

---

1 www.aifs.gov.au/cfca.

2 www.copmi.net.au.

divisions, units and departments within individual state and territory governments. Increasingly these entities are funding non-government and community-controlled Indigenous agencies to provide child protection interventions for vulnerable families, including preventive interventions. Contemporary child protection systems are significantly limited in their abilities to prevent harm to children, because they are typically designed to respond once harm has already occurred.

They are also limited in their ability to reach children who are living in potentially harmful home environments (e.g. in the homes of the more than half-a-million parents using illicit substances, or as one of the nearly 100,000 children presenting at homelessness services) but who have not been reported as such, and to engage with parents in a way that is non-stigmatising and non-threatening. Because of the immense demand and strain on statutory child protection systems, governments are more likely to fund research that focuses on the statutory responsibilities of governments in the response to abuse and neglect, rather than invest significant amounts in research focusing on effective prevention strategies and therapeutic service options. Currently the evidence for effective interventions is drawn from overseas and it is not known to what extent these might be effective for Australian children, families, workers and systems.

Australian research, in common with other jurisdictions, has highlighted the highly complex needs and chaotic circumstances that can make families vulnerable – characterised by alcohol and drug misuse, parental mental health problems and high levels of conflict and violence (Bromfield *et al;* Dawe and Harnett 2013a; 2010; Mildon and Shlonsky 2011). Child protection research has been characterised by an abundance of knowledge describing the phenomenon of child abuse and neglect, and the family and social circumstances in which it arises. Far less is known about how to intervene with vulnerable children and their families. There is urgent need to enhance the outcomes for vulnerable children and families (Delfabbro *et al.* 2010a; Productivity Commission 2014).

Research from Australia and the US has also identified that the vast majority of practitioners in children's services systems do not use evidence-based interventions, and where they are used, they are often adapted or changed, potentially losing the key components of effective interventions (Forman *et al.* 2009; Lewig *et al.* 2010). Further impacting on the ability for practitioners to undertake 'evidence-based practice' is the quality of the evidence base to inform practice decisions. Audits of Australian out-of-home care (Cashmore and Ainsworth 2004) and child protection (encompassing child abuse prevention and child protection) (Higgins *et al.* 2005; McDonald *et al.* 2011) research have been undertaken. Cashmore and colleagues (2006) published a paper synthesising the audits and discussing the findings in terms of 'what had been done' and 'what needed to be done'. The key issue highlighted in the audits was an overall shortage of research and funding for research, leading to an inability to claim an adequate evidence base for sound policy and practice or to be able to single out research priorities (Cashmore *et al.* 2006).

Auditing child abuse prevention programmes (rather than research), (Tomison and Poole 2000) found that most of the many prevention programmes in Australia reported some process evaluation data. However, there was insufficient outcomes data to determine 'what works'. In an international review of prevention programmes, only 5 of 52 programmes identified were Australian programmes (Holzer *et al.* 2006).

The audits have provided a first step in determining what has been done. However, systematic reviews are required for more detailed information about what is known from Australian research and to assess the quality of this research. A review of the out-of-home care research concluded that the research is largely of 'good quality' (e.g. methodology adequately described, sample size and design were appropriate to the research question) but that there was an overreliance on qualitative methodologies and the quantitative research only provided descriptive data (Bromfield and Osborn 2007). The result is an evidence base rich in detail but with limited capacity to be generalised to other groups or contexts. Regarding the use of international research, the authors cautioned that the applicability of these findings needed to be tested in the Australian context. Looking forward, Osborn and Bromfield (2007) identified the importance of cross-jurisdictional studies together with longitudinal research and practice evaluations to improve the capacity to generalise findings.

Building a national research agenda

A number of research frameworks have been developed to guide future research on child abuse and neglect across the world (Institute of Medicine and National Research Council 2014; Macmillan *et al.* 2007). These frameworks have explored different aspects of child protection systems (e.g. out-of-home care), or attempts to better inform preventive and response efforts. Many have used a public health framework to frame the areas for research efforts (Scott 2006), highlighting the need for epidemiological or population-based research, aetiological research, intervention and evaluation research, and data on implementation and dissemination (Bromfield and Arney 2008, p.10).

There have been several recent developments in Australia that aim to identify research priorities of greatest relevance to child protection policy and practice, and to provide easy access to current research findings. These include, first, the *National Framework for Protecting Australia's Children* – a national policy initiative, taking a public health perspective, and endorsed by all heads of Australian federal, state and territory governments – which has identified national indicators for measuring progress towards a society in which child abuse and neglect is prevented, as well as indicators against standards for out-of-home care (Council of Australian Governments 2009).

Second, a priority action of the National Framework has introduced is the *National Research Agenda* (Department of Families Housing Community Services and Indigenous Affairs together with the National Framework Implementation Working Group 2011), accompanied by a searchable database of Australian child protection research and evaluation projects[3]. The aim is to identify areas for which there is a need for an evidence base to fill a high priority gap in policy or practice knowledge. The research agenda builds on national studies of the knowledge needs of practitioners, policy makers and researchers in the field of child protection (Bromfield and Arney 2008), as well as critical research gaps identified by national experts at various national forums from 2006 to 2009 (e.g. National Child Protection Forum). The development of the research agenda was guided by a range of principles, highlighting amongst others, the importance of evidence for 'what works', making children and young people the focus, dissemination and communication. The core agenda is classified according to a range of themes from prevention, intervention and coordination and delivery of services. Specific topics include, for example, community attitudes and engagement in the prevention of child maltreatment; the impact of chronic maltreatment and cumulative harm; and decision-making regarding placement of children into care.

---

3 http://apps.aifs.gov.au/cfcaregister.

The National Research Agenda states that there is an overreliance upon qualitative methodologies and identifies specific methodological priorities, as well as the areas of research mentioned above, including longitudinal research, data linkage and cost-benefit analysis. Further considerations include the improvement of data collection (e.g. standardised administrative data, inclusion of child maltreatment in longitudinal studies) to make data more reliable, accessible and nationally comparable. Collaborative efforts are also highlighted as a means to enhance the relevance and quality of research (in this applied setting). The National Research Agenda has received little in the way of additional resourcing (only $600,000 has been committed over three years (2011–14) to fund three new research projects).

Third, Australian research efforts in the field of child welfare are being further supported by the Royal Commission into Institutional Responses to Child Abuse and Neglect (Royal Commission) instituted in 2013. The Royal Commission identifies four broad areas for research, to include, amongst others, response and justice for victims. Research that helps the Royal Commission to understand the context of its work and to fulfil its terms of reference has been prioritised, including identifying the existing systems and structures for responding to abuse, examining the findings of previous enquires and exploring the history of relevant institutions and practices. The Commission's Interim Report (Royal Commission into Institutional Responses to Child Sexual Abuse 2014) documented the completion of 21 projects (for the full list see the Interim Report[4]). A further 12 projects are ongoing, and overall 52 projects may be completed as part of the Royal Commission.

The Interim Report highlights the necessity of building upon the research and that recommendations need to be developed that are practical, necessary and targeted. Simply conducting the research isn't sufficient; the Royal Commission into Institutional Responses to Child Sexual Abuse suggests 'evaluating, analysing and consulting on our research projects to test theories, findings and proposed solutions before using them as the basis for any recommendations' (2014, p.202).

Bringing together Australian child protection research

In addition to a specific focus on child sexual abuse within institutions, the Australian evidence base has recently grown in a range of critical

---

4 www.childabuseroyalcommission.gov.au/about-us/reports.

areas of child protection practice and policy. Dedicated efforts to examine the factors driving child protection involvement for children and their families has helped us understand *patterns of contact with the system*: the alarmingly high levels of contact for all children with child protection systems. For example: the fact that in South Australia approximately one in five children will be the subject of a child protection notification by the time they are 15 years old) (Delfabbro *et al.* 2010b); the gross overrepresentation of Aboriginal and Torres Strait Islander children across every facet of our child protection systems (Australian Institute of Health and Welfare 2014; Delfabbro *et al.* 2010a; Guthridge *et al.* 2012); the concerns that bring refugee families into contact with child protection and how those concerns could be ameliorated through earlier intervention with families (Lewig, Arney and Salveron 2010); the extent to which children's chronic involvement with child protection services is associated with poor outcomes and requires alternative responses to investigative interventions (Bromfield, Gillingham and Higgins 2007).

To understand *vulnerability*: the degree to which alcohol and other drugs may be a factor in children entering out-of-home care (Jeffreys *et al.* 2009), and effective interventions for families in which substance misuse is a problem (Dawe and Harnett 2013a); identifying 'hidden' populations of children whose needs may not be considered in service delivery, such as children of incarcerated parents (Saunders and McArthur 2013) or children whose families may be accessing homelessness services (Gibson and Morphett 2011; Moore and McArthur 2011).

To understand *out-of-home care*: the factors driving the growing number of children entering out-of-home care placements (Tilbury 2009), and the characteristics of successful family reunification efforts (Delfabbro *et al.* 2014); understanding how out-of-home care experiences impact upon children (Bromfield and Osborn 2007; Delfabbro, King and Barber 2010); better understanding parental experiences of child removal and the factors that support contact between children in care and their biological families (Salveron and Arney 2013; Salveron, Lewig and Arney 2009); alternative approaches to carer recruitment and retention and the use of kinship placements in child protection (McGuinness and Arney 2012).

There has been a concerted effort by Australian health economists to identify 'best bets' for interventions and policy directions to prevent child abuse and neglect and to provide effective responses (Segal, Dalziel and Papandrea 2013). This research has also focused on the effectiveness of home visiting approaches as a preventive intervention (Dalziel and Segal 2012).

Other emerging areas of research are examining the extent to which interventions that use extended families and other families within neighbourhoods as agents of change might be effective in preventing and responding to child abuse and neglect, particularly for Aboriginal families (Blacklock *et al.* 2013; McGuinness and Westby 2012; Schulman, Curtis and Vanstone 2011).

Just as descriptive research has identified risk factors for children's safety and wellbeing (such as adult mental health problems, parental substance misuse, domestic and family violence and parental homelessness), so also Australian researchers have examined how adult service sectors might better identify and respond to the needs of children and work collaboratively across traditional sector boundaries (Scott 2009). This research has included studying the factors that promote or inhibit child-centred practice and policies in multidisciplinary practice models for adult mental health and child protection services (Arney, Lange and Zufferey 2010; Darlington and Feeney 2008), homelessness and drug and alcohol services (Dawe and Harnett 2013a; Gibson and Morphett 2011) and national efforts to enhance service sector responses (McDougall and Gibson 2014).

Finally, research has begun to examine the extent to which promising practices and programmes may be implemented at scale in Australia. Studies using 'diffusion of innovation' theory[5] and implementation research frameworks to examine the transplantation of new ways of working in different service environments have found high levels of variability in the use of evidence-based programmes and practices (Lewig *et al.* 2010; Mildon and Shlonsky 2011). National research mapping of curricula in universities across Australia has found that in the disciplines of psychology, social work, nursing and midwifery and education, many tertiary education programmes do not cover topics relating to child abuse and neglect, child safety or wellbeing, unless it is in the context of legal responsibilities such as mandatory reporting requirements or presenting evidence in court (Arnold *et al.* 2008; Parry *et al.* 2009). This research has led to work to enhance undergraduate and postgraduate teaching through changes in national standards in curricula for social work and

---

5 Diffusion of innovation theory explains the spread of knowledge about new programmes and practices and describes the factors influencing the decision-making regarding the uptake and implementation of these new approaches in different contexts.

nursing and midwifery courses, and the development of resources to support teaching and learning in this area (Briggs *et al.* 2010).

There still remain a number of 'grand challenges' for child protection research, questions that can only be answered through a national search for solutions that includes significant investment, multiagency input and cross-jurisdictional coordination. Bromfield and Arney (2008, p.12) identify the research opportunities offered by the multi-jurisdictional nature of Australian child protection policy development and practice. Common issues can be examined across jurisdictions, which can support natural experiments through comparative methods.

It is hoped that enhancing the collective knowledge base regarding child abuse and neglect will result in an increased development and implementation of evidence-informed policy, practice and programmes in prevention and protection. This may also enhance the return on investment and serve to leverage increased investment of public, private and philanthropic funding. Ultimately, the aim is to enhance the responsiveness of workers, organisational systems, families and carers to the needs of vulnerable children.

Conclusion

There has been an increasing focus on child protection research and research translation in the Australian child protection and child welfare context over the past 15 years (Bromfield and Arney 2008). Driven in part by a greater desire for 'evidence-based' policy and practice, governments and the non-government sector have invested to establish national research and dissemination organisations (Mildon *et al.* 2012). In the last decade, we have seen stocktaking and assessment of the extent and quality of the Australian evidence base ultimately resulting in the creation of a national research agenda informed by the knowledge needs of practitioners, policy makers and researchers across the country (Bromfield and Arney 2008; Bromfield and Osborn 2007; Cashmore *et al.* 2006; Department of Families Housing Community Services and Indigenous Affairs together with the National Framework Implementation Working Group 2011; Higgins *et al.* 2005; McDonald *et al.* 2011).

The results of stocktaking and quality assessment in the areas of child protection and out-of-home care in 2004–05 highlighted an overreliance on qualitative research and gaps in rigorous evidence across multiple areas of practice to inform 'what works'. This situation continues, but progress is being made. Organisations are working to make better use of administrative data in identifying children and young people who may be at particular risk in their systems, and evaluative and experimental studies have begun to identify effective interventions for families with complex needs such as drug and alcohol misuse, family violence and mental health problems, as well as being used to study the impacts of child protection reform efforts (Arney *et al.* 2010; Dawe and Harnett 2013a; Guthridge *et al.* 2012).

The needs of specific populations of children (e.g. Aboriginal and Torres Strait Islander children, children from refugee backgrounds, children of incarcerated parents) and potential family- and community-based strategies to address these needs have been the subject of research (Delfabbro *et al.* 2010a; Delfabbro, King and Barber 2010; Lewig, Arney and Salveron 2010; Saunders and McArthur 2013; Schulman *et al.* 2011). Increasingly, research that prioritises children's voices and their participation is being conducted to inform significant policy reform efforts (e.g., responding to child sexual abuse, practice reform in child protection frontline work) (Cashmore 2011; Moore and McArthur 2011; Royal Commission into Institutional Responses to Child Sexual Abuse 2014).

While these developments are promising in the Australian child protection landscape, there is still an urgent need for research that identifies the scope of child maltreatment in Australia, for large-scale prevention studies and for research that examines optimal approaches for multidisciplinary initiatives to protect children. This chapter highlights the importance of a national framework for research in child protection and points to the benefits from targeted multi-jurisdictional and international research collaborations. Finally, to 'search for a solution' to reduce child abuse and neglect and to enhance our community and system responses, research requires the combined wisdom of researchers, practitioners, policy makers and community members.

CHAPTER 9

Advances from Public Health Research

Melissa O'Donnell

The World Health Organization (WHO) estimates that at least 18 million children in the European Region will suffer from child abuse and neglect during their childhood (Sethi *et al.* 2013). Infants and young children are at greatest risk, especially within low- and middle-income countries, and in those where higher economic inequalities exist (Butchart *et al.* 2006). Despite government efforts to reduce child abuse and neglect, a study of high-income countries/regions (Sweden, England, the US, New Zealand, Western Australia and the Canadian province of Manitoba) found no consistent evidence for a decline across a range of child abuse and neglect indicators, including violent deaths, child abuse-related injury hospital admissions and child welfare agency contacts (Gilbert *et al.* 2012).[1] While it is difficult to get estimates of the true extent of child abuse and neglect due to issues of disclosure and determining whether injuries were accidental or intentionally caused, what is known is that child abuse and neglect is preventable and can be reduced (Krug *et al.* 2002).

---

1 The authors do observe that an alternative explanation for the data could be an overall decline offset by increased recognition and recording.

Public health approach to child abuse and neglect

A major challenge in preventing child abuse and neglect is that traditional child welfare services normally focus on intervening once abuse and neglect have occurred. Interventions tend to provide for children at highest risk and further along a pathway towards alternative care. By comparison, in the area of communicable disease it has long been recognised that intervening only once there has been an outbreak of a disease is not an effective or efficient means of reducing mortality and morbidity. Since the late 1990s there has been a growing interest in a public health approach to violence-related injuries including child abuse and neglect. WHO advocates a need to adopt a public health approach to the prevention of violence, emphasising the importance of protecting children from harm in the first instance (Krug *et al.* 2002).

What is a public health approach

A public health approach is grounded in epidemiology – that is, the study of how a disease is distributed in populations and factors that increase or reduce the risk of developing it. Historically, one of the most famous examples of epidemiological research and a public health approach is John Snow's work during the 1850's London cholera outbreak (Snow, Frost and Richardson 1936). Snow had theorised that cholera was transmitted through the water supply and to prove this he mapped the cluster of cholera cases in relation to the water pumps in the affected district. His research showed that the cases of cholera were centred on the now famous Broad Street pump; he used this evidence to convince the local council to disable the pump, subsequently ending the cholera epidemic in that area.

A public health approach to child abuse and neglect comprises four steps:

1. Surveillance – defining and monitoring the magnitude of the problem.

2. Identification of risk and protective factors – establish why abuse and neglect occur, using research to determine the causes and the factors that increase or reduce the risk of abuse and neglect.

3. Develop and evaluate interventions – determine what works to prevent abuse and neglect and for whom, by designing, implementing and evaluating interventions.

4. Implementation – implement interventions in a wide range of settings by scaling up effective interventions. The effects of these interventions on abuse and neglect rates and risk factors need to be monitored to evaluate their impact and effectiveness.

(Modified from Krug *et al.* 2002)

Public health interventions

Interventions in a public health approach are aimed at risk and protective factors within the child, family and community. They can be classified into three different levels of intervention. The first level is primary (or universal) interventions, which are strategies that encompass whole communities and all families. Media campaigns to educate the public on child safety (e.g. 'shaken baby syndrome'), universal maternal and child health clinics, available in many countries, and parental leave payments to support parents in the early stages of a child's life are all examples (O'Donnell, Scott and Stanley 2008). Universal prevention initiatives have the potential not only to prevent abuse and neglect but also to enhance overall child health and wellbeing. While many areas of primary intervention have not had significant research into their effectiveness, the universal parenting programme of 'Triple P' has had significant evaluation and shown evidence to reduce population-level indicators of child abuse and neglect (Prinz *et al.* 2009).

Secondary or targeted interventions are aimed at families and children where there is a risk of abuse and neglect. Some universal intervention programmes have the ability to identify vulnerable families early enough to avoid a path to child abuse and neglect. Maternal and child health clinics often utilise screening tools to identify mothers who are exhibiting symptoms or are at risk of postnatal depression and refer them to specialised services (Beyondblue and Perinatal Mental Health Consortium 2008). A number of countries utilise respite care for parents who need support in raising their children, particularly for those children who have disabilities (Boddy *et al.* 2009; World Health Organization Regional Office for Europe 2010).

Tertiary interventions will always be necessary, even with well-resourced primary and secondary interventions. These interventions include treatment for abused children to reduce the impact of trauma and formal statutory intervention by child welfare agencies including the removal of children to temporary or permanent alternative care.

The current challenge for many child welfare agencies is responding to families at lower levels of risk to prevent child abuse and neglect or their reoccurrence (Gilbert et al. 2009; Scott 2006). Many countries are now implementing differential response models (Gilbert et al. 2012). This involves providing preventive services to families assessed at low or moderate levels of risk of child abuse and neglect. At present there is limited evidence about the effectiveness of the models, with researchers calling for more rigorous methodological testing (Kyte, Trocmé and Chamerberland 2013; Waldfogel 2009). However, what is promising is that recognition of the need for alternative approaches is being recognised.

Population-level record linkage – the key to an effective public health approach?

Estimating the magnitude of child abuse and neglect is an essential first step in a public health approach. Achieving this in child abuse and neglect research is often more challenging since it is not as straightforward to measure as other communicable diseases or conditions. Definitions of child abuse and neglect vary internationally and even states/provinces within countries may have definitional differences (Fallon et al. 2010). A further challenge in measuring child abuse and neglect, assuming consistency of definition, is that children and parents may be unwilling in surveys to disclose abuse or neglect, and even in retrospect inconsistencies in disclosure are found (Fergusson, Horwood and Woodward 2000).

Epidemiological research methods utilised in public health often involve large-scale cohort studies to determine prevalence of a disease, potential risk factors and outcomes in terms of morbidity and mortality. They can be expensive to implement and it can be difficult to recruit some of the most vulnerable children and families (Stateva et al. 2006). For these reasons and more there has been a growing interest in using and linking routinely collected administrative data records held on individuals by public health and social services for research. Record or data linkage is the bringing together from two or more different sources data that relates to the same individual, family, place or event (Holman et al. 2008). Population-level record linkage is a key strand in epidemiological research. There is growing recognition in some countries of the value of routinely collected government administrative data for research that can establish the magnitude of a range of child wellbeing problems, identify determinants, consider possibilities for policy and practice development and evaluate any changes (Magus *et al.* 2006; Putnam-Hornstein *et al.* 2011; Roos *et al.* 2008).

Cross-agency data

Population record linkage primarily uses health databases including hospital morbidity, mortality data and birth registrations, although the scope has now broadened to include social care data, with many countries linking child welfare data, education data, etc. Traditionally, research on child abuse and neglect has relied upon child welfare agency data, often confined to information on referrals or notifications of suspected and/or confirmed cases. Linking to other government administrative data extends the range of indicators of child abuse and neglect that can be monitored in research. These indicators can include health data, for example to monitor hospital admissions resulting from intentional injury or neglect, and education data to determine numbers of children suffering from educational neglect through chronic attendance issues. Linked routine government administrative data can also be used to identify risk and protective factors associated with abuse and neglect, such as children's birth characteristics including pre-term birth, disability, parental age at birth, etc. Parental hospital morbidity data can determine the size and extent of groups at high risk such as those with substance use issues, domestic violence and mental health issues.

Examples of research using cross-agency data

Child abuse and neglect are not the sole responsibility of child welfare services. Interagency data enable researchers to investigate indicators of maltreatment, risk and protective factors and both short- and long-term outcomes across government agencies to deal with this multifaceted issue. Examples of the types of indicators that have been investigated include: child abuse and assault-related hospital admissions and emergency department presentations (Gonzalez-Izquierdo *et al.* 2010; O'Donnell *et al.* 2012; O'Donnell *et al.* 2010a); child homicide and assault-related deaths in mortality registers (Gilbert *et al.* 2012); and rates and types of allegations of child abuse and neglect and substantiated allegations in child welfare agency data (O'Donnell *et al.* 2010b).

Gilbert *et al.* (2012) argue that comparing trends in child abuse and neglect indicators across six different countries/regions provides a natural experiment to understand the impact of differing policies and practices.

They drew upon routinely recorded data sources and standardised definitions in each county to examine variation in maltreatment measures and whether any differences in occurrence were true differences, possibly linked to policy or an artefact of the methodology employed. They investigated trends in indicators of child abuse-related deaths, hospital admissions and child welfare agency contacts and compared the prevalence across countries. They found that across six developed countries/regions (Sweden, England, the US, New Zealand, Western Australia and the Canadian province of Manitoba) these indicators were predominantly stable or showed increases over time with large differences in incidence rates across the countries/regions. Sweden in comparison with the US showed lower levels of child abuse and neglect indicators, which is consistent with lower rates of child poverty, parental risk factors and the provision of universal support for parents in Sweden.

Putnam-Hornstein *et al.* (2011) linked child protection service records with birth record data in California State, US, for all children born between 1999 and 2002 up to age five years, to identify population-level rates of maltreatment; 13.9 per cent of children were referred on account of possible maltreatment before the age of five, with 5.2 per cent identified as substantiated victims of maltreatment. Racial disparities were apparent, with children born to black mothers more likely to be reported to child protective services at 29.7 per cent, in comparison with children of white mothers at 13.4 per cent. Children more likely to be referred to child protection services also included 17.9 per cent of children with a health risk present at birth, one in three children born without established paternity, and 25.4 per cent of children born to teenage mothers. Putnam-Hornstein *et al.* (2011) state that by identifying these high-risk groups in the population at birth we can readily target them for preventative services at an early point.

In Western Australia, longitudinal health and birth data were linked to investigate drivers in the rise of child maltreatment allegations. An increase in the prevalence of prior mental health disorders for parents was found between 1990 and 2005 (O'Donnell *et al.* 2013). There was a 3.7 per cent increase per year in the risk of children being born to a mother with a prior mental health disorder, from 76 to 131 per 1000 births, and for fathers there was a 3.1 per cent increase per year from 56 to 88 per 1000 births. There was also a 4.7 per cent increase per year in the risk of children being born to a mother who had a recent mental health contact in the last 12 months prior to birth. Similarly, there has been a marked rise in the number of children born with neonatal withdrawal syndrome due to maternal substance use in pregnancy (O'Donnell *et al.* 2009). There was a 16.4 per cent yearly increase in children born with neonatal withdrawal syndrome, with 35 per 10,000 births diagnosed in 2005. These children had a high risk of substantiated child abuse and neglect in the first year of life and were over ten times more likely to be taken into out-of-home care.

As the data collected by government agencies involved in population-level record linkage is often from a state or country, it is possible to use this data, for geographical mapping of areas and to determine community-level factors that may impact on child maltreatment. Utilising spatial data, Freisthler *et al.* (2007) found that increases in off-premises alcohol outlets was related to an increase in rates of child maltreatment in that area. They also found that rate of entry into foster care was related to the number of bars in local areas and determined that regulating alcohol outlet density may be a viable community intervention in reducing child maltreatment. Geographical mapping and spatial analysis allows the identification of areas where child maltreatment indicators are showing high prevalence. This information can be used by government agencies to direct services and intervention strategies.

Another important use of the linked data is to examine outcomes for children involved in child welfare services. Research from Canada on child maltreatment and emergency department presentations for suicide-related behaviours has shown that children removed from their homes for maltreatment were over five times more likely to have a first presentation for suicide-related behaviour than their peers. This was found for both sexes after controlling for socio-demographic characteristics, mental health service use and emergency department presentations (Rhodes *et al.* 2012). Linked cross-agency data provides the opportunity to investigate educational, health, mental health and juvenile justice outcomes for children in out-of-home care or families who are provided in-home services. If longitudinal data are accessible, then potentially the impact of policy or practice changes can be traced.

Observations

What is vital in the use of population-level linked data is the protection of individual privacy. Governments do not make direct operational use of linked population-level data; the data is linked only for research purposes, and the data that researchers receive is de-identified with names and addresses of individuals removed. This is essential for community and government support of this type of research. The protocols and procedures employed by the Data Linkage Branch within the Western Australian Department of Health to link cross-agency data are now accepted as international best practice (Kelman, Bass and Holman 2002).

There are four main advantages of using population-level record linkage in child maltreatment research: first, it is relatively low cost, as it is using existing and available data; second, capture of total population data; third, inclusion of multiple birth cohorts allowing longitudinal analysis; and fourth, as data is de-identified, the privacy and identity of the individuals is protected.

The main disadvantage concerns limitations in the data that agencies collect (Brownell and Jutte 2013). While some datasets capture almost the entire population, such as birth and death registrations and all hospital admissions, other datasets are only available for children and families who have contact with specific government agencies. There may be restrictions in areas in which government services are limited, where families are not accessing services or families have not come to the attention of child welfare services. Not all factors associated with child abuse and neglect are captured by the agency databases, such as parenting styles and child temperament. With consent, information obtained from survey and cohort studies can be linked to routinely collected administrative data to provide a more complete picture. In Western Australia, the process of using de-identified linked data has enabled research on sensitive issues, such as maternal drug use in pregnancy, parental mental health issues and child protection outcomes (Trutwein and Rosman 2006).

Utilising government agency data provides an opportunity for researcher–agency collaboration. Working in partnership, government agencies and researchers may be better able to develop collaborative research plans important for policy and practice in child maltreatment. This may support a greater use and translation of research findings. The involvement of the community in research processes is vital in order to legitimate (or not) the acceptability of using population data for specific studies. This is important for public information and public confidence in recognition of the expanding use of publicly held data for research.

Community members can be strong advocates for public engagement with research where they see potential benefits.

A public health approach advocates earlier intervention and the provision of universal support to reduce family and community vulnerabilities to child abuse and neglect, and to identify children and families who require more targeted intervention to reduce the risk of harm. It is imperative to collect good quality data to quantify this problem and to monitor the effectiveness of interventions and their implementation.

PART 3

Challenge Three: Working with Children and Families

CHAPTER 10

Integrating Family Support and Child Protection in Child Neglect

Brigid Daniel

Across the UK child neglect has become the most common reason for child protection referrals, and operational categories of neglect represent the majority of registrations and reasons for child protection plans in all UK jurisdictions (Burgess *et al.* 2014). It has been estimated that this represents only a small proportion of the numbers of children who are experiencing a distressing and damaging level of unmet need (Cawson *et al.* 2000; Daniel *et al.* 2013a; Radford *et al.* 2011). It has long been recognised that the kind of incident-driven, forensically oriented child protection systems that characterise the UK and other countries with similar jurisdictions are not necessarily suited to providing the best service to neglected children and their families (Buckley 2005; Daniel 1998; Stevenson 1998). There appears to be a systematic failure to get to the heart of the problem of neglect despite many reviews of the system and attempts to develop different configurations of services (Children's Improvement Board 2012; Munro 2011b). This chapter will explore the suggestion that this failure springs, in part, from the difficulty organisations, systems and individual practitioners have with integrating family support with protective responses, in short, with providing authoritative responses. It draws on a body of research on neglect that reflects the current status of the evidence base.

Research base

A systematic review of the literature on noticing and helping the neglected child (Daniel, Taylor and Scott 2009a; Daniel, Taylor and Scott 2009b; Daniel, Taylor and Scott 2010) was carried out according to systematic review guidelines (Centre for Reviews and Dissemination 2007). A total of 63 papers published in English between 1995 and 2005 that relied on research were included; many of the studies were small in scale, looking back in time and relying primarily on qualitative information. Two studies met the criteria associated with the randomised controlled trial (RCT). Few studies set out to study professional recognition of and response to neglect as their primary aim. No common definition of neglect was found and many findings conflated child abuse and neglect as 'maltreatment', making it difficult to disentangle neglect as a distinct concept. A majority of studies concentrated on risk factors that predisposed or were associated with child neglect. The review identified that professional assessment should focus on the accumulation of stressors in a family and incorporate an historical element to increase recognition of neglect.

An in-depth review of the situation in Scotland (Daniel, Burgess and Scott 2012) was based on a combination of data, including published statistics, survey questionnaires sent to a small number of key specialists, telephone interviews and 15 multiagency focus groups across six areas in Scotland. Also of interest was the inclusion of findings from an earlier UK-wide poll undertaken by YouGov in 2011 of the general public and professionals, which included questions about child neglect. The harm caused by child neglect to childhood development was identified across professions, although perhaps more surprising was the extent of concern by the general public about the significance of neglect for children growing up in the UK today. Building increased capacity to link the various kinds of data relevant to the recognition and treatment of neglect kept by different specialist agencies across Scotland was identified as improving aggregate information.

Action on Neglect was a specific project that encouraged practitioners to develop solutions to the barriers that stopped them providing help to neglected children and their families (Burgess *et al.* 2013). It established a year-long knowledge exchange project with three groups of practitioners and managers working with children in England. Special emphasis was placed on the views and experiences of children themselves, bearing out the idea, that children have their own definitions of what constitutes child neglect.

A series of ongoing UK-wide reviews of neglect and responses to neglect (Burgess *et al.* 2014; Burgess *et al.* 2012; Daniel *et al.* 2013b) focus exclusively on child neglect, drawing on the viewpoints of the different groups of individuals involved – the practitioners, the policy makers, the children and their families and the public. The single focus on neglect in a series of publications captures a rounded picture of the consequences of child neglect and how to improve professional engagement: for example, the identification of multiple barriers (in descending order – funding, the gap between child and adult services, lack of services, the point at which access to services is set and so on) professionals, especially social workers, report facing when trying to help neglected children and their families (Burgess *et al.* 2014).

Finally, there is a considerable history of interdisciplinary research to develop models that match parenting approaches/styles with positive (and negative) outcomes for child development. Baumrind's (1972) model of four parenting styles research linked authoritative parenting, as below, with better child outcomes and the model of warmth with clear boundaries has become the accepted touchstone for parenting and compatibility with the developmental needs of children.

- Authoritative parenting – is warm but firm, sets standards for behaviour and uses rational sanctions with explanation.

- Authoritarian parenting – establishes obedience and conformity by the use of punitive discipline without explanation or discussion.

- Indulgent parenting – is accepting of most behaviour, characterised by passive discipline and few demands on behaviour.

- Indifferent parenting – centres on parent rather than child needs, and in the extreme is neglectful.

The practitioner's dilemma

Currently there are two potentially incompatible discourses about child neglect that do not necessarily provide a coherent framework for practice in recognising and responding to child neglect. One discourse is driven by the recognition that the parents of children who are formally identified as neglected are amongst some of the most materially and emotionally deprived: they are likely to have experienced neglect or abuse in childhood; they are affected by mental health problems, learning disabilities, substance misuse and domestic abuse; and they are the hardest hit by policies that exacerbate inequalities in society and, therefore, require empathic and supportive responses (Cleaver, Unell and Aldgate 2011; Featherstone, White and Morris 2014). The other discourse is driven by the recognition that neglect is highly damaging to children in the short and long term. It is associated with the risk of significant harm or death; it is not necessarily caused by poverty; and it can be intractable and is, therefore, a serious child protection issue (Narey 2014). It is not surprising that practitioners struggle with finding the right balance in the face of these different perspectives.

Organisations struggle to create optimal systems for responding to the full range of support and protection needs in situations of neglect. The common response has been to establish systems that require children with unmet needs to be categorised as either 'children in need' or as 'children at risk', who are then offered a different type of service, usually differentiated as 'family support' or 'child protection'. Legislative instruments in the UK have set up the conditions for these bifurcating pathways. It is easy to see why such arrangements have developed as a way of managing high numbers of children who are identified by nurses, doctors, police and teachers as needing some kind of professional intervention. But, for many children who are neglected, practitioners struggle to find sufficient evidence to justify forensic investigations. Although the legislation and associated child protection arrangements do appear to be relatively effective in reducing child deaths and improving outcomes for children subject to child protection plans (Devaney 2004; Devaney *et al.* 2013; Sidebotham, Atkins and Hutton 2012), they are not particularly helpful when it comes to providing the kind of rounded responses needed for child neglect. International comparative analyses show that many other European countries are oriented towards a family welfare and support approach (Gilbert, Parton and Skiveness 2011; Hill, Stafford and Green Lister 2002; Parton 2014).

What is clear about neglected children is that they are both 'in need' and 'at risk'. The risks to children's development and safety flow from the extent to which their needs, including needs for protection, are unmet. Practitioner time and organisational resources can be devoted to trying to decide along which of the two pathways – in need or at risk – a child should be sent, when in fact they would benefit from aspects of both pathways. The fulcrum at the centre of the support and protection balance is parental capacity and willingness to change. When working with neglect it is crucial to assess, and monitor on an ongoing basis, the precise level of professional authority that is required to ensure that the child's life improves, and to avoid:

- long-term support that the parents like but that leads to no appreciable change in the child's life; or

- heavy-handed and overly intrusive state intervention, which, at its extreme, entails unjustified removal of a child from home.

Horwath and Morrison's (2001) model offers a two-dimensional framework for making sense of parental motivation and willingness to change within a timeframe to match a child's developmental trajectory, which is especially important in cases of child neglect. The model evaluates levels of effort and of commitment, which, when combined, give four categories. These categories also offer insights into the level of compulsory professional authority that may be needed and include: *genuine commitment,* where parents make good efforts to change and show commitment to improving their parenting for the benefit of the children – there is unlikely to be a requirement for compulsory measures; *tokenism,* where parents express commitment to change, but for a range of possible reasons do not put in effort to change – there may be a need for compulsory measures, although the parents may be able to accept that the care is not good enough; *compliance imitation* or *approval seeking,* where there can be high effort to make changes (perhaps sporadically) but the commitment to sustained change is not demonstrated – there may be a requirement for compulsory measures to ensure sustained effort; *dissent* or *avoidance,* where there is a combination of low effort and low commitment – compulsory measures are likely to be required.

Harnett (2007) has developed, for use in child protection work a procedure for dynamic assessment of capacity to change, which pays particular attention to objective measurement of changes in parenting (Dawe and Harnett 2013b, pp.12–13). It is always important to gauge the extent of change for the better in the child's life, whether providing early intervention or crisis intervention and whether providing 'family support' or 'child protection'. A key message from research is that families where there is neglect need both protective support and supportive protection.

Protective support

Neglecting the structural

The term 'neglect of neglect' has become common currency in discussions about child neglect (Wolock and Horowitz 1984). However, it is the first part of the paper's title ('Child maltreatment as a social problem') that is as relevant today as when it was written. The child protection system has consistently failed:

- to recognise the extent to which poverty and deprivation elevate the likelihood of neglect; and

- to take proper account of the effects of poverty and deprivation when working with families.

Poverty and parenting

Not all poor people neglect their children but poverty certainly does not help (Featherstone et al. 2014; Hooper et al. 2007). This has become even more salient with the onset of reductions in public expenditure in the UK in the past four years and associated welfare changes that are impacting on children and their families who 'will serve as the shock absorbers of society' (Family and Parenting Institute 2012, p.2). Households with children are disproportionately affected by a cap on benefits introduced in 2013, with more than 175,000 affected (Action for Children 2014). The rollout of Universal Credit, a single monthly benefit to replace a range of existing benefit payments, may well exacerbate problems because individuals will be expected to apply for and manage their account online and receive monthly payments, including housing costs, into a bank account. Parents who are already struggling to manage their finances are likely to find this especially challenging.

Fiscal measures are considered to impact differentially to increase inequalities between rich and poor. Inequalities are known to be significantly corrosive for individuals and societies (Wilkinson and Pickett 2009). Reforms of welfare and benefits systems are predicted to have greater impacts on areas where people with the greatest need live: 'One of the reasons why some places are so poor is that they have so many people claiming benefits [...] And just how much harder will the reforms hit the poorer parts of Britain than more prosperous areas?' (Beatty and Fothergill 2013, p.4).

Bywaters (2013) argues that there is the need for a far more detailed and robust consideration of the issue of inequalities in child wellbeing and protection. This is especially relevant to child neglect. He argues for a body of research into child welfare inequalities akin to the burgeoning field of health inequalities. This argument appears to be supported by the fact that the financial loss in the geographical areas most affected by welfare reform is twice the national average for a working adult but in areas least affected by welfare reform it is about half the national average (Beatty and Fothergill 2013).

There are also inequalities in access to routes out of welfare dependency, such as moving into employment or moving area, which can be seriously hampered by lack of employment opportunities and low housing stocks. These suggested ways out may especially affect parents of neglected children, who can lack qualifications and/or can be affected by factors that may impair their capacity to find and sustain paid employment.

Whilst it is true that not all parents living in poverty neglect their children, there is an undoubted association between poverty and neglect, which can be attributed to a complex interaction of factors exacerbated by living in poverty (NSPCC 2008; Spencer and Baldwin 2005). To parent effectively in situations of poor housing, meagre income, lack of local resources and limited educational and employment prospects requires a high level of organisation and determination: '[P]arents who […] have very limited parenting skills are often attempting to meet the needs of their child in a context that even the most competent parents would find challenging' (Horwath 2007, p.38).

Of the professionals from all key disciplines who responded to an online survey in the review of neglect (n=243) (Burgess *et al.* 2014) 66 per cent gave 'greater poverty/deprivation in the area' as their top reason to account for increases in suspected child neglect.

Policy consequences – parents' views

In the review (Burgess *et al.* 2014), parents gave many examples of the ways in which social policies, most notably those concerning income support, public housing and public spaces, had made life more difficult for them: 'It's really hard to manage on the money even if you're working. If you're a single parent with one child you are better off working, but if you have more than one child you're not' (Burgess *et al.* 2014, p.14).

Parents said that they had to be made homeless to get on the list for housing and that it took many months to move from a hostel to a private, then council let. There were many concerns about the impact of the spare room subsidy, known colloquially as the 'bedroom tax'. In summary, this means that claimants of housing benefits receive a reduced amount of benefit towards housing costs if they are considered to have more space than they need, leading to concerns about the potential disruption of having to move to smaller accomodation and the associated loss of social networks. Some parents described the neighbourhoods they lived in as 'scary' and often risky for children:

> Our area is not one which you could let the kids play out by themselves. One park has a warden, which is fine, but others are strewn with needles and broken glass and teenagers often use the parks at night. (Burgess *et al.* 2014, p.14)

Children, when asked, did not comment directly on the significance of poverty for themselves, but they were aware of the impact on parents.

Professional views

Not only are cutbacks in public spending in the UK during a period of economic downturn directly affecting families, they are also systematically reducing the capacity of systems to respond effectively to parents whose problems tip them into the zone of requiring professional help. In particular, it is the family support approaches that are most likely to be eroded. Following year-on-year funding cuts, the Local Government Association (LGA) for England expressed concerns about the significant pressures the funding gaps will put on children's social care (Local Government Association 2013).

Practitioners (n=1552) who responded to the online survey (Local Government Association 2013) clearly felt that cuts were eroding their capacity to help neglected children and their families and that the situation would only get worse. 'Lack of resources' was noted as a key barrier to providing help. Thirty-five per cent thought spending cuts had made their situation more difficult (up from 29% in an earlier survey in 2012), while 43 per cent thought it would be more difficult in the future. Of those surveyed it was social workers who reported having been hit hardest by public spending cuts, with nearly two-thirds saying such cuts had made it more difficult to intervene. Seventy-three per cent said public spending cuts would make it more difficult to intervene in future. Over half of the police officers agreed with this, saying spending cuts would make it more difficult to intervene in cases of suspected child neglect.

The interaction of poverty and neglect is complex and impacts on support and protection in a number of ways. Child welfare and protection systems need to find effective ways to deal with large numbers of referrals of families affected by social changes. This can lead to tensions between the universal services of health, education, housing, income support and statutory social services. It is difficult for practitioners to know how best to deal with entrenched poverty whilst still maintaining a focus on the needs of children for love and care. The economic and fiscal climate within which professionals are trying to implement the policies of early intervention and prevention that are so important for reducing the numbers of children experiencing damaging neglect of their needs is harsh. Hooper *et al.* (2007) undertook a study to explore the relationships between the experience of poverty, effects on parenting and impact on child wellbeing. They interviewed 70 families from areas of both high and low deprivation including families who were in receipt of family support services and social services. The study included exploration of the interaction between poverty and child neglect. They found that parents believed that professionals saw 'neglect' when the problem was really poverty. Professionals, on the other hand, were confident that they could discern the difference. However, the study found that, whilst increased money might not always solve the parenting problems, poverty 'often slipped out of sight' (Hooper *et al.*, 2007, p.109). Instead, professionals tended to focus on parental factors at the expense of consideration of the impact of wider structural inequalities.

Empathic support

Featherstone *et al.* (2014) make the compelling argument that child protection practice needs to take proper account of the wide-ranging effects of poverty, deprivation and inequality of opportunity. They suggest that the system has become so child oriented that it has lost sight of the needs of parents. They call for empathic support, based on relationships, which places 'care' rather than 'risk' at the heart of intervention. They are clearly espousing a family support approach, whilst recognising that children do need protection.

Parents value the kind of emotional and practical help provided by family and parenting support workers often employed by third-sector agencies: 'They could show empathy about the causes of our difficulties'

(Burgess *et al.* 2014, p.37); 'My family support worker just sat and listened and asked "How can I help?" rather than telling me what I needed – or what they thought I needed' (Burgess *et al.* 2014, p.35).

There can be a misperception that interventions labelled as 'family support' (often delivered by the third sector) are a separate activity from 'child protection'. However, to be effective, family support has to include attention to the child's needs for protection. One example of this kind of protective support is Action for Children's UK Neglect Project, which was part of a five-year Intensive Family Support (IFS) programme delivered from Action for Children projects in selected sites across the UK. IFS is a whole-family approach that includes comprehensive assessment, parenting programmes and intensive home visiting. There is a focus on forming relationships with families, even those who have had difficult or hostile relationships with other service providers. An independent longitudinal evaluation of 85 cases showed that in 79 per cent there was prevention of neglect or improvement in the level of concern about neglect. In only 21 per cent was there no improvement. However, perhaps the most crucial finding was this: 'The ability and willingness on the part of parents to engage with services was a crucial factor in deciding whether progress would be made or children removed for accommodation' (Long *et al.* 2012, p.6).

Supportive protection

It has been known for decades that chronic neglect can lead to some of the poorest outcomes of all forms of maltreatment (Egeland 1991; Egeland, Sroufe and Erickson 1983). Serious case reviews are multidisciplinary reviews undertaken in England into cases of child death or serious injury when abuse neglect is known or suspected. A recent and detailed analysis of serious case reviews through the lens of neglect demonstrated just how dangerous this can be for children. In 139 reviews (2009–2011) neglect was present in 60 per cent of them. Although uncommon as the main cause of death, neglect was a factor in the majority of deaths related to maltreatment (Brandon *et al.* 2013). Children who experience neglect, therefore, need to be protected from the likely significant harm that can ensue.

In an earlier analysis of serious case reviews Brandon *et al.* (2009) identified what they called the 'start-again syndrome' in which repeated attempts to support families to parent successive children are tried and fail – thus suggesting a failure to assess fully the capacity to change.

Building on a previous study of outcomes for neglected children removed from home (Farmer, Sturgess and O'Neill 2008), Farmer and Lutman (2010) examined the outcomes for 138 neglected children who had been returned home after a period of being looked after away from home. Of these, 110 children had already been followed for two years; 20 more were added to the sample and all were followed for a further three years. They showed that startlingly little attention is routinely paid to addressing the factors that affect parenting capacity and that precipitate children being removed from home in the first place. This means that children are returning home to the same or worse circumstances.

Although the parents who took part in Action on Neglect (Burgess *et al.* 2013) were appreciative of family support, they were also aware of the need for protective responses:

> But we'd like you to know that, even though it can be a pain at the time and we may really hate you when you're on our backs, some of us look back and think that the threat of Child Protection Plans and having our children taken away did make a difference to us and made us get our act together. (Extract from a letter from parents to practitioners, Burgess *et al.* 2013, p.20)

Children and young people can also be very perceptive about their own parents' capacity to change and can also identify the limitations of family support approaches that lack authority:

> Some of us had family support for years and years and it didn't really help us much. Please respect our views if we don't want to have this sort of help […] Some parents can change and others can't. Some are given too many chances and we are left too long at home. (Extract from a letter from young people to practitioners, Burgess *et al.* 2013, p.17)

Family Drug and Alcohol Courts (FDACs) exemplify supportive protection to address situations of entrenched substance misuse where there is a risk of infants being accommodated away from home. The intervention involves a multidisciplinary team, which adopts a problem-solving method. A tailored package of support is aimed at addressing the full range of problems affecting parenting, coupled with clarity about what has to change by when – all overseen by the same judge within the court process. An independent evaluation (Harwin *et al.* 2011) showed that 19 (48%) of the 41 mothers who had gone through FDACs stopped using substances, compared with 39 per cent of 19 comparison mothers who went through standard court procedures. The children of 39 per cent of FDAC mothers were living at home, compared with 21 per cent of children of comparison mothers. Importantly, especially when considering the effects of neglect, swifter decisions about permanent placements were made for children whose parents were not able to respond to the intensive package of support.

Conclusion

There is an overriding conclusion to be drawn from the research that informs this chapter on child neglect. In families where neglect is identified by formal systems, childcare and protection needs often coexist alongside poverty and other life challenges. The key message from research is the need, where neglect is present, to combine protective support and supportive protection, in other words to integrate family support and child protection. Individual practitioners need to be supported to offer the combination of authority, compassion and empathy that leads to authoritative practice. Practitioners in universal and statutory systems should seek to avoid an artificial separation of need from risk. Aspects of support and protection can be distributed across the multidisciplinary network, as long as there is careful planning and communication to ensure that the aims of all are congruent.

Acknowledgements

Cheryl Burgess (University of Stirling) and Jane Scott (WithScotland) have been fundamental to the development of the empirical and conceptual material in this chapter. Action for Children funded the UK-wide reviews of neglect, which were undertaken in partnership with Kate Mulley and Hannah Dobbin (Action for Children). The Economic and Social Research Council funded Action on Neglect, which was also undertaken in partnership with Action for Children with contributions from David Derbyshire and Erica Whitfield (Action for Children) and Julie Taylor (University of Edinburgh).

CHAPTER 11

Relationships in Practice
'Practitioner–Mother Relationships and the Processes that Bind Them'[1]

Lorraine Waterhouse and Janice McGhee

This chapter pares down practitioner–mother relationships in child protection social work to analyse their significance and the assumptions that bind them. In social work the concept of relationship has proven durable, reproduced between generations of its writers (Biestek 1957; Butrym 1976; Cooper and Lousada 2005; Forder 1966; Hamilton 1940; Howe *et al.* 1999, 2010; Perlman 1957; Ruch, Turney and Ward 2010; Stevenson 1986). Historically, individual freedom to grow formed a common principle (Perlman 1957) contained in the functions of the formal organisation (Perlman 1957; Towle 1946). The typical way in which relationships form is by a non-judgmatic approach, confidentiality, a neutral but understanding response and a relationship that could be used to some advantage by the person. There is no break with the idea of taking account of the impact of social forces on the individual and their social circumstances.

---

1 This chapter is abridged, with permission from Wiley, from the following article: Waterhouse, L. and McGhee, J. (2013) 'Practitioner–mother relationships and the processes that bind them.' *Child and Family Social Work.* Article first published online: 30 April 2013, DOI: 10.1111/cfs.12074.

Three reasons underlie our focus on practitioner–mother relationships. First, the central place allocated to women in current child protection processes; second, the importance attached to maternal care in society; and third, disaggregating 'parents' in order to examine in depth one set of relations to better understand the nature of the whole from first principles. In child protection the striking feature of practitioner–mother contact is a dual professional obligation to assist parents and children and a public duty of child safety surveillance. We think Judith Butler's (2005) book *Giving an Account of Oneself* and her theory of recognition is crucial for the understanding of relations between parties of unequal status and resource.

In child protection social work contact is often not voluntary, which contributes to parental resistance to engagement with practitioners (Forrester, Westlake and Glynn 2012). Intervention may be considered more punitive than supportive in its purpose (Lapierre 2010). Fear of losing care of their child becomes an overriding concern leading to wariness about seeking assistance (Humphreys and Absler 2011). Morally, women may be blamed for alleged failures in the upbringing and protection of their children and at the same time women are perceived as the 'main alternative source of child protection' (Scourfield 2001, p.83). Howe (1994, p.524) observes that women comprise the majority of social workers and clients. The fact of involvement takes on a symbolic significance where an accusation of want of good mothering hangs in the air and remains in an undecided state while containing the potential to crystallise into an indictment. Judith Butler (2005) provides a philosophical and linguistic theory to conceptualise what lies beneath practitioner–mother contact in child protection.

Judith Butler

Judith Butler is Maxine Elliot Professor of Rhetoric and Comparative Literature, University of California, Berkeley. In her book *Giving an Account of Oneself* (2005) she examines notable philosophers of the 19th and 20th centuries, especially Adorno (1963), concluding that their differences are overshadowed by a common theme. She is concerned with the problem of ever knowing who we are. She writes on the moral and ethical issues that arise in constituting 'I'. The 'I' derives from giving an account of oneself and what we have done (Butler 2005). The demand to account for oneself, she argues, 'is a matter of fathoming at once the formation of the subject (self, ego, moi, first-person perspective) and its relation to responsibility' (Butler 2005, p.135). Butler questions whether we can ever be self-knowing when our very emergence remains opaque to us. It will always miss the constitutive beginnings. This unknowing has its origins in early relations, primary relations, not always subject to consciousness. The knowledge of partial transparency binds us as people to each other and is a resource of ethics. The terms in which we give an account of ourselves are in part social in character, the 'impress of social life' (Butler 2005, p.135). Therefore, the ethics of responsibility must include a social as well as rhetorical critique, where the self cannot be set apart from our social life.

Butler puts in plain words the emergence of self when she writes: 'I begin my story of myself only in the face of a "you" who asks me to give an account'. In this encounter 'we must become self-narrating beings' (Butler 2005, p.11). This narrative capacity is the prerequisite for any account of moral agency and it is through this narrative capacity that we find a means of giving an account of ourselves and assuming responsibility. This is not the same as telling a story about oneself. The difference lies in the self-questioning acceptance of the possibility of causal agency. This is the very essence of the creation of self as a reflexive subject: 'I come into being as a reflexive subject in the context of establishing a narrative account of myself when I am spoken to by someone and prompted to address myself to the one who addresses me' (Butler 2005, p.15).

An account, to be recognisable as such, takes place within 'the structure of address' regardless of whether the 'addressee' is present or explicitly identified (Butler 2005, p.36). In giving an account, individuals try to make themselves recognisable and understandable. This begins with a narrative account set within a social existence beyond the individual. In this way social norms frame an encounter between self and other. This constitutes the scene of recognition, the backcloth for 'seeing and judging who I am' (Butler 2005, p.29). Butler cites Cavarero (2000) who suggests the fundamental question to recognition is 'who are you?' (Butler 2005, p.31). This question assumes individual uniqueness that cannot be fully apprehended by the other, thereby limiting reciprocal recognition. In other words, there are inbuilt limits to knowing ourselves and knowing others.

Butler suggests the question of ethics emerges 'precisely at the limits of our schemes of intelligibility, the site where we ask ourselves what it might mean to continue in a dialogue where no common ground can be assumed' (Butler 2005, p.21). This builds on Arendt's politics of relations where 'exposure and vulnerability of the other makes a primary ethical claim upon me' (Arendt 1958, cited in Butler 2005, p.31). In Butler's terms, giving an account is 'a kind of showing of oneself, a showing for the purpose of testing whether the account seems right, whether it is understandable by the other, who "receives" the account through one set of norms or another' (Butler 2005, p.131). Judging is a form of address. Prior to judging another, we must be in some relation to them. The relation will inform the ethical judgements we finally make.

Butler (2005) accepts that judgements are necessary for political, legal and personal reasons. She recognises that problems of power arise and should cause us to ask of ourselves, '[H]ow ought I to treat you?' (Butler 2005, p.25). Social recognition sometimes obligates us to suspend judgement in order to apprehend the other. She goes on to argue that it may only be under conditions of suspended judgement that we create the conditions necessary to render us capable of an ethical reflection on the humanity of the other. The point she makes is that suspended judgement is needed when we are least able to understand the other and their actions, namely, when these arise at the outer periphery of human behaviour – human annihilation. She explains that, notwithstanding the necessity of judgements, not all ethical relations are reducible to acts of judgement. It is possible to judge without recognising the individual; judgement is not a theory of recognition as elucidated by Butler.

Outright condemnation without recognising our common humanity and without asking the question 'Who are you?' deprives us of an ethical recognition of the individual's personhood. It also deprives us of knowing what humans are capable of doing to themselves and others. This 'knowing' allows us to prepare ourselves for or against things that may happen. Condemnation is the way we make the other unrecognisable and can work against self-knowledge and self-disclosure.

A rhetorical dimension is intrinsic to giving an account of oneself. The individual is responding to the premises of the other and seeks to influence the other's view of them and their actions. This is not deliberate deception but arises from the limits of human self-knowledge and suggests the importance of 'generosity to the limits of others' (Butler 2005, p.80). This recognition must become inherent to moral judgements otherwise there is a risk of a kind of violence to the ethics of speaking *with* another about their actions. Butler is neither abdicating individual responsibility nor holding individuals to account for their actions. Her theory of recognition incorporates the idea that we can never fully know ourselves because our identity encompasses a pre-speech history and the stamp of social life.

In giving an account to the other, a complex interaction is taking place. The self is constituted and reconstituted within social relations both formal and informal. In any conversation the individual responds to the reactions of the other and this contributes to the shaping of their account. In this interaction the process of giving an account of oneself causes a 'certain rupture' with the self, as elements of the 'I' 'do not bind together' (Butler 2005, p.69). This brings the potential for individual harm as well as individual growth and in either case does not return them to the same position as before. It brings 'hope' that the other will be able to make sense of the different threads of their account and will offer it back to them in a new form that does not absolve responsibility but retains the integrity of an 'I'. This brings responsibility for the connection with the other, especially in the context of an unwanted address and is the nucleus of an ethical claim each to the other.

Discussion

Butler helps us to see there is more than meets the eye to the practitioner–mother encounter. Her philosophical critique points to the problem of ever knowing who we are and the ethical dimensions present in every human encounter. While the emergence of self and the consequences for self-knowledge may remain open to other interpretations, Butler provides a language to think about the essence of what happens when one person addresses another. This holds special resonance for practitioner–mother encounters in the case of child protection social work, given what is at stake.

The scene of address concerns women as the potential cause of harm to their child either through acts of commission or omission for which they are to accept responsibility (including harm that may be done to a child by others). This accountability is twofold: first through a system of justice and punishment for their actions or inactions; and second, through legal disposals that may remove the child from their care. The women are being asked by an established authority, in this case represented by social work on behalf of the child protection system, to give an account of themselves as mothers for the wellbeing of their child.

This background raises inevitable tension between the need to establish meaningful practitioner–mother relations when the reasons for contact may provoke fear and threat for both parties. Butler's formulation of the scene of address, the demands of giving and receiving an account of self and the ethical claim this imposes to prevent violation of the other provide a theory for explaining and analysing the roots of this tension. Children experience a number of risks to their wellbeing. Douglas (1966, p.xix) suggests 'naming a risk amounts to an accusation'. In child protection, women must give an account of themselves as mothers. They must defend against the accusation of child maltreatment, qualify it or accept causation.

Butler discusses Nietzsche's (1969) argument that moral accountability only follows an accusation. He suggests individuals give an account of themselves because someone with delegated power from a system of justice where a threat of punishment is present has asked them to do so. This causes us to reflect through fear and terror. For these reasons alone we become conscious of ourselves only after some injury has been inflicted and when someone suffers as a consequence. A representative of authority, in a position to mete out punishment, seeks to find the cause of the suffering by asking of another if they might be the cause. This makes the individual reflect upon him or herself for two reasons: first to question whether by their actions or inaction they may have caused suffering; and second, whether to take responsibility for these actions (*or inaction*) and their consequences. It is through this process we become morally accountable and reflective beings, constituting the subjective 'I'.

Butler provides an alternative conceptualisation of what it means to give an account of yourself neither based on the wish to punish by a legitimate authority nor prompted by fear in the individual. She suggests being addressed by another carries other valences besides fear. She describes a narrative form of knowing and narrating that provides, in essence, a non-coercive account of the coming into being of the reflexive subject, the 'I'. The story of self originates only in the face of a 'you', whether present or in the mind, who asks 'me' to give an account. To know and be known requires us to become self-narrating beings.

Telling a story about oneself is not the same as giving an account of oneself. Giving an account depends on four elements: first, a capacity to set out events sequentially; second, to connect these events coherently and convincingly; third, to draw upon a 'narrative voice and authority' for an audience; and fourth, for the purpose of persuading them. This narrative capacity is the prerequisite for any account of moral agency — an account of whether we caused injury and take responsibility.

The implications of this approach for practitioner–mother encounters are non-trivial. The interaction is immensely complex and has the potential to constitute 'a linguistic and social occasion for self-transformation' (Butler 2005, p.130). Herein lies the possibility of creating an ethos in child protection practice that provides an ethical foundation to address the mothers as women in their own right and as reflexive self-narrating beings. Butler identifies the importance of communication that does not evoke fear or terror but instead conveys an ethics of equality between the two parties. This ethos is captured when she writes: 'spoken to by someone and prompted to address myself to the one who addresses me' (Butler 2005, p.15). In this way she alerts us to two possibilities: first, the creative potential for women to engage with practitioners as reflexive subjects through establishing a narrative account of themselves; and second, the potential for ethical harm through a failure to respect the women's individual personhood.

For creative potential to be harnessed it needs to be recognised that the women are being asked to do something that is highly risky for themselves and potentially for their children. First, no assumption can be made that state intervention is without iatrogenic effects on the lives of the children. Women may be as concerned to protect their children from the state as the state may be to protect children from their parents. Brown (2006, p.368) found that women took deliberate steps to offset the 'risks inherent in the child protection system itself'.

Second, there are inbuilt limits to knowing ourselves and knowing others – a common predicament for us all. This brings foreignness to the self and in turn places a limit to narrative accountability (Laplanche 1999).

Third, the profound implications for the women and their legitimate fears of what lies before them and their child at the other side of self-questioning and self-disclosure need to be acknowledged. The development of the mother–infant bond is a complex process and demands an integration of contradictory feelings towards the child. To give an account of themselves as mothers they must accept the possibility that the self has causal agency. Frosh (2011, p.54) underlines that 'stating one's feelings is a complex process at the best of times'. Cases of alleged child abuse and neglect are not the best of times. In essence the women are facing an existential fear that their account of themselves may render them unrecognisable by others and as significantly unrecognisable to themselves (Agamben 1995).

Asking women to make themselves objects of possible knowledge brings an ethical responsibility to the form of address in face-to-face encounters in child protection. The ethos to this form must take as its starting point an awareness of self-limits and a generosity to the limits of others. In giving an account to practitioners women may hope the fragments of their story may be linked together and given back in some new form. This ethical connection between practitioners and women brings the potential for self-knowledge and self-development and the potential to benefit the child.

Our capacity to reflect upon ourselves – to tell the truth about ourselves – is also limited by what is and is not 'speakable' within the discourses and social norms of the day (Butler 2005, p.21). Ideas about women as mothers influence the organisation of child protection practice and vice versa. There is rarely a need for physical force but there is an overriding necessity for women to do two things in the system: first, they must give an account of themselves as mothers; second, this account must earn them the status of 'good mother' within the public systems. Failures on either count risk personal and parental autonomy.

When the interests of children are paramount in law, policy and practice, those of all other parties are by definition secondary. There is no doubt that some children are harmed by the actions and inactions of their parents. Social work is committed to ethical standards where public interest comes first – to act as officers of the court, to keep public trust, to apply technical expertise for conflict resolution and to avoid scandals. The current child protection policy and legal context does not encourage social workers to act autonomously as social advocates for wider social interests despite the centrality of advocacy and social mediation to the ideology and history of social work. The scope for offering pragmatic help to any problems raised is limited. The arrival of a social worker in a household now appears to signal a potential threat to the mother's autonomy and identity.

Butler's theory of recognition alerts us to the importance of supporting the narrative capacity of women caught up in child protection processes and of allowing the mother to give an account of herself as a woman and as a mother. Recognition obligates practitioners to be able to suspend judgement in order to apprehend the other, in this case the mother, as fully as possible. It has to be more than a way to get to the child and has to respect the woman. Recognition reflects an egalitarian, non-threatening register and offers women an opportunity to narrate an account of themselves in their own terms, as they are are often struggling to survive in distressed social and economic circumstances.

Research suggests that mothers are evaluated across a number of factors. These include: her impact on the child; her care of the child's body in neglect cases; her capacity to put the child first; and her capacity to protect her child from the father/male partner (Featherstone 1999; Scourfield 2001). Sykes (2011) carried out empirical work to understand mothers' responses to accusations of child neglect in a rural Michigan county. She found that mothers developed a number of strategies to resist being classified by the state as 'neglectful mothers'. The mothers she interviewed, like almost all mothers, needed to preserve their identity as good mothers and protect it from being spoiled (Sykes 2011, p.449). Mothers need to be confident that they will get a fair deal – that the norm of fairness is applied and that their child will benefit from what they tell the social worker. Conditions need to be created that allow women to speak frankly about their philosophy of childrearing and their direct experience of raising their own child.

Butler opens up fresh possibilities in conceptualising practitioner–mother relations when she recognises what it means to be asked to give an account of self that is prompted by neither fear nor a wish to punish. We argue that to realise a non-coercive narration, a child protection framework must be formulated that has at its core an ethics of equality. Under such a framework the orientation becomes asking women to give an account *of* their childrearing rather than asking women to account *for* their childrearing. This is the very opposite of abdicating individual responsibility. The beginning of moral agency depends on the creation of conditions for a narrative capacity that is not founded on fear. We suggest that the question 'Who are you?' has to be the starting point for practitioner–mother relations. This supports self-recognition, self-knowledge and the recognition of the other.

CHAPTER 12

Emotional and Relational Capacities for Doing Child Protection Work

Andrew Cooper

This chapter discusses how emotions affect relationships in modern child protection work. It takes account of the nature of the task, the varying emotional capacities of practitioners, the organisational context in which the work is undertaken and managed and the wider social and policy context, which may influence organisations and individuals.

The chapter's main themes are congruent with the comprehensive and systematically researched model of child protection work developed by Barlow and Scott (2010) in which 'relational theory' informs and is informed by 'relationship-based practice' as central elements of the conceptual underpinning for a '21st century model of safeguarding' (p.36). Here I focus on the experiential and relational demands of the child protection role and the associated needs of practitioners, while offering signposts to other literature that readers may wish to read in the original.

In child protection work rapid assessments and decisions need to be made, each implying possible longer-term decisions of profound and irrevocable consequence – the temporary or permanent removal of children from their families; the sometimes intense conflicts surrounding these actions and decisions and a reality of painful uncertainty about such decisions. Were they 'right' for the child and his or her long-term future, or was the parent actually 'right'?

In some respects 'child protection' is a misleading name for the work, which always entails engagements with families, or systems of 'care', within which vulnerable or at-risk children and young people are living. Many public inquiry reports, and more recently the Munro Review of Child Protection (Munro 2010, 2011a, 2011b), have highlighted the importance of social workers' skills and confidence in relating directly to children, especially young children. But between the social worker and the child sit the adult parents and carers. Meta-analyses of serious case reviews (Brandon *et al.* 2012) consistently reveal a trilogy of factors most frequently associated with cases of serious maltreatment – domestic violence, serious mental health problems and drug and alcohol dependency. But whether all, some or none of these are features of a particular case, another factor will almost invariably be present, namely a complex, difficult and emotionally charged set of parental or carer family histories.

Responsibility, anxiety and defences

Skilled and experienced child protection practitioners carry an immense weight of responsibility for their work and live with anxiety about the decisions they must make that concern the temporary or permanent removal of a child, the risks to children on their caseloads who may remain inadequately protected over time and the suffering that children are enduring. Often, practitioners are frightened, because a proportion of families with whom they work have members who are threatening, violent and dangerous, and these cases exert a disproportionate influence on the mind and work of child protection practitioners. These professionals need and deserve confident and sustained organisational support in order to sustain their ability to do the work over long time periods, to maintain professional confidence in themselves and for the wellbeing of the children and families with whom they work. Their organisations and managers are frequently under economic pressure and a range of expectations bear down on modern public services, which often seem to be making good practice harder while claiming to do the opposite – harsh and arbitrary performance and inspection regimes, unrealistic timescales for assessment and decision-making, efficiency and productivity targets that are often euphemisms for resource reductions and perpetual 'churn' in the policy environment.

These external factors, which occasion organisational anxiety and defensiveness because they can be experienced as a threat to organisational survival or credibility, often intersect with the anxieties arising from the primary task itself to produce a particular fear-laden 'structure of feeling' in child protection services that is indeed challenging. Cooper and Lees (2014), drawing on the tradition of thinking originated by Menzies Lyth (1988) about social systems as a defence against anxiety, as well as recent research into the emotional life of frontline child protection teams, argue that modern organisational contexts generate new forms of professional anxiety. The nurses and nurse managers in Menzies Lyth's original study of a general hospital were shown to be anxious about the potential for physical and emotional harm to patients entailed by their routine tasks. Defensive behaviours against this anxiety often took the form of 'ritual task performance' and 'upward delegation' of decision-making and responsibility in a way that became formally inscribed in the organisational system. Lees' (2014) research revealed similar patterns of anxiety and defensiveness in child protection teams, but in addition the impact of inspection regimes and performance management targets also gave rise to intense anxiety, not about 'doing harm' to service users but about external judgements of professional failure, incompetence or culpability that might result in injury to the professional 'self' of the workers and their organisations. These two forms of anxiety are different in important ways, but the defensive behaviours elaborated to cope with them had very similar qualities. Cooper and Lees comment:

> Hence the familiar and oft-repeated observations about contemporary defensive organisational practices being directed towards 'covering your back'. What is implicitly lamented here is precisely the replacement of concern (albeit anxious concern) for the patient or service user, by a dominant anxiety for the survival of the professional self. (Cooper and Lees 2014 p.244)

And yet, people choose to do this work, sustain their commitment to it over many years and, given the right blend of training, reflective supervision, opportunities for personal and professional development and robust enough organisational conditions, find immense satisfaction in it – fulfilment for their sense of vocation and professional integrity. A senior practitioner in one of the teams researched by Lees commented: 'You're very often taking the weight of the world on your shoulders' (Lees 2014, p163). He was probably unaware that he was echoing the title of a book of the same name by the French sociologist Pierre Bourdieu, in which he interviewed ordinary working-class people and professionals in order to disclose the depth and intensity of 'social suffering' that they bear on behalf of the rest of society, usually without public or social recognition. Bourdieu remarked of social workers that as 'agents of the state' they are 'shot through with the contradictions of the state'. In particular, he noted the contradiction between 'the endless missions entrusted to them' and 'the invariably paltry means granted to them' (Bourdieu 1999, p.184).

The two primary tasks of child protection work

Child protection work is mostly undertaken beneath the surface of public or even political awareness, except of course on those occasions when an alleged 'failure' explodes into the public and media domain. The idea that there are two 'primary tasks' in child protection work, one that is about actually protecting children from harm and the other that is about protecting the rest of society from everyday awareness of the prevalence and proximity of child maltreatment, is important because it helps make sense of the continual backdrop of anxiety attending the first primary task – protecting children – which is always enacted in the shadow of the second – the fear of public humiliation, exposure and scapegoating when a 'scandal' breaks the surface. These ideas are more fully explored in Cooper (2014) but are well summarised in this quotation from an English local authority manager:

> [W]e're paid to stop the public from knowing that this sort of stuff goes on. So when the public find out about it, they get angry because they're denying that people do this stuff to children. And therefore if it becomes exposed they've got to blame somebody – 'how dare you invade my living-room at six o'clock when the news is on with this horrible stuff'. (Cooper and Whittaker 2014, p.260)

So, what makes it possible to tolerate the demands of child protection work and even to flourish and find fulfilment in the work? The remainder of this chapter will address this question, by keeping the experience and professional capacities of the practitioner firmly in view, but also by recognising that contexts of practice shape experiences for better or worse.

Core skills and capacities

I propose there are a number of core relational and emotional skills and capacities required of child protection practitioners. Here these are explored from an experiential perspective, with references to useful research and literature.

Facing difficult truths and feelings

Practitioners need an emotional and intellectual readiness to face extremely discomforting, disturbing, emotional truths about what might be happening to children in families or other care systems, and not to turn away from feelings, signs and observations that point towards the possibility of serious abuse. Few of us are really comfortable with the thought or the feeling that we may be in the presence of violent, damaging, sexually aggressive or neglectful behaviour. The younger and more vulnerable the child, the more this discomfort may intensify. Equally, in relation to older children and adolescents, we may rationalise our suspicions of maltreatment by thinking of the young person as 'almost an adult'. This theme of both 'seeing and not seeing' what is in front of our own eyes is explored in more depth in Cooper (2005), and Rustin (2005), two papers written in the aftermath of the Victoria Climbié inquiry in an effort to make sense of some lessons for practice and policy not addressed by the inquiry report. Cooper (2005) and Munro (2011a) have emphasised that the question to ask is 'How and why did competent people seem to have been unable to see and do the obvious in this situation?'. This is a question that demands serious analytical thought, rather than a flight into blame and accusation. The answer is not straightforward and Munro's (2011a) and others' (Stevens and Cox 2008) discussions of 'complexity' in child protection work are important. However, Burton's (2009) review of decision-making and the role of supervision notes that 'Managers should continuously promote an ethos of openness, rigour and challenge' in order to engage a 'fresh pair of eyes' (p.14).

Making sense of difficult experiences

A capacity to make sense of frightening, distressing, perturbing feelings and thoughts aroused in the worker by direct contact with children and their families is centrally important. Making meaning out of emotional experiences of this kind, as a way of building a picture of 'what it is like for children to be inside this family' is always a provisional matter, and while it cannot usually be the only basis for decision-making, it is an essential part of the process. The experience of undertaking an infant or young child observation, supported by small reflective seminar groups, is invaluable in developing this capacity for unflinching observation of both children's experience and development in a family, but also of the mind and 'self' of the practitioner as she or he is emotionally engaged in intense observational and practice experiences. This method of training, which originated at the Tavistock Centre in London, has formed part of some social work training in recent years, and its contribution to practitioner confidence and skills has been researched and evaluated. Urwin and Sternberg's (2012) collection offers a way into this area with many accessible papers that describe the value of observational experience. One study of the impact of infant observation on social workers' development reported here found that at two-year follow-up participants felt their practice had changed and that infant observation 'had increased their understanding of children, families, and themselves' (Urwin and Sternberg 2012, p.42).

Understanding family and system dynamics

Practitioners need to develop an understanding of the distinctive relational dynamics of different family systems, how these impact emotionally on the practitioner and how inevitably she or he will be drawn into these dynamics. Systems of 'care' can be thought of as lying somewhere on a spectrum. At one end are closed systems that reject help and may operate like a 'gang', responding to the worker as a threatening and dangerous presence. At the other end, there may be real willingness to engage, but a sense of 'stuckness' develops and the worker becomes immersed in a long relationship that feels burdensome or futile, with a powerful dynamic of aimless dependency. In between are many other possibilities, including those where parents angrily demand 'help', but only on their terms, rejecting what the worker offers, until the next crisis when the pattern is repeated. Marion Bower's (2005) paper offers a deeper account of this theme with powerful case illustrations, while Mattinson and Sinclair's (1979) study of frontline practice is a neglected classic that sympathetically and vividly evokes the dynamic strains of working with difficult families. As Bower says, commenting on one case example, it is important to be aware:

of the way in which the interactions of family members function as a defensive organisation, and the pressure on the social worker to enact a role which fits in with the organisation, in this case a figure who is rejecting or abusive. (Bower 2005, p.159)

Building and sustaining relationships

The ability to work with and understand relationships between children and their carers and sustain these relationships is obviously key. Many children who are vulnerable or at risk are not removed from their families. 'Thresholds' for intervention shift constantly, and many families move back and forth between different organisational categories of concern and action. In the interests of the children, the worker needs to be capable of sustaining relationships with the whole system of care, which is likely to include extended family members and other professionals. Tensions and conflicts about child protection interventions may be present between parents and professionals, or between professionals, and resentment about continuing agency involvement is common. But such tensions are an inherent part of the 'the case' and first need to be assimilated as part of the task if they are to be constructively tackled. A central source of tension in worker–family relationships is the fact that many carers of children at risk are perfectly aware of the inadequacy of their parenting but feel profoundly guilty or ashamed, intensely vulnerable to criticism and fear the consequences of professional involvement. They may not find it easy to admit their anxieties to themselves, let alone to a child protection practitioner, who may exercise statutory authority and holds power over family life.

To be curious about the family story

A simple way of starting to manage parents' and carers' anxieties about their own care, and the reality of professional involvement, as well as gaining vital understanding of the meaning of any suspected abuse, is for the worker to be curious and enquiring about the parents' or carers' own stories of their childhoods and parenting. All parents have a story. To show genuine curiosity about these histories is not to evade the need for a focus on the welfare of the children, except in circumstances of emergency. Rather it is to engage the carers in a process of empathic 'sense making' of the very situation that has brought them to professional attention. Once revealed, the links between how abusive or neglectful parents relate to their children, and how they were parented themselves, are frequently striking and transparent to everyone. But often no one has previously thought to ask and to encourage reflection on these matters. The power of the 'ghosts' that haunt the family script and the transformative potential of exploring them is wonderfully articulated in Fraiberg, Adelson and Shapiro's classic (1975) paper. A focus on children as a part of their families, rather than just the child, is part of the 'relational' model advocated by Barlow and Scott (2010).

Using reflective supervision – the importance of containment

In my experience, any group of social workers discussing their work and organisations will soon enough turn to the question of supervision. A lack of reflective supervision focused on understanding the case and the emotional and relational challenges it presents, the encroachment of 'managerial' supervision on the reflective space and the decline in supervisory skills among social work managers are some of the most pressing issues for contemporary child protection practice. Part 1 of the Munro Review of Child Protection is strong on this point, and notes:

> To work with families with compassion but retain an open and questioning mindset requires regular, challenging supervision. The emotional and intellectual demands on social workers are substantial; this and their need for high quality supervision and support has been accepted by the Social Work Task Force. (Munro 2010, p.18)

Toasland's (2007) paper addresses the important link between the positive emotional and relational conditions that support children's healthy development and the parallel provision of reflective and containing supervision for professionals working with parents who may not be able to offer this and may not have received it themselves. 'Containment' is the interpersonal, psychological process of receiving difficult, anxious, disturbing or unacceptable emotional communications from another person, tolerating them, becoming able to think about them and then finding ways to resume communication with the other person so that, for them, these states of mind become, in turn, more manageable, tolerable and 'thinkable'. Many of the children with whom child protection practitioners work have not enjoyed a reliable or consistent enough experience of this kind with their parents or carers, who in turn have often been denied it for themselves and thus transfer their struggle on to professionals, not necessarily with awareness. Such unprocessed emotional communication is contagious, in the sense that it may be transmitted from person to person until someone succeeds in making emotional and cognitive sense of the feelings and thoughts involved – or not.

While Toasland's (2007) paper on the importance of social work management providing 'containment for the container' is a helpful point of entry to this area, because frontline child protection work, via processes of projection of the kind just outlined, often leaves practitioners feeling ashamed, as though it is *them* who are inadequate, blameworthy, failing, wrong and even abusive, seeking supervisory help is not always straightforward. None of us are likely to be comfortable at revealing such anxieties, self-doubt, and erosion of self-confidence to a colleague, especially a manager. In my experience of training with experienced practitioners, it is the provision of non-judgemental, thoughtful, small-group 'work discussion' spaces (Bradley and Rustin 2008) that they find most valuable in 'detoxifying' their experience of the work. Agency provision of good supervision is vital, but reluctance to avail oneself of it may be as important in its breakdown as managerial neglect, and so the 'management' of supervision must take account of this dynamic.

Managing in relation to your colleagues and agency

From my experience, an unacknowledged truth about most people's working lives is that what keeps them awake at night is tensions and conflicts with colleagues and managers, as much as anxiety about the work itself. Child protection workers do carry a continual burden of worry about their caseloads, and their organisational worries add to this. There is a long and helpful tradition of research and writing that tries to understand the nature of organisational tensions and conflicts by looking at how these mirror or represent 'enactments' of the conflicts and anxieties present in the dynamics of the service user systems themselves (e.g. Bacon 1988; Mattinson and Sinclair 1979), as well as how systematic defences arise in organisations to protect staff from too much anxiety about the work. Recent studies of child protection teams (Lees 2014; Whittaker 2011) show that 'delegation upwards' from frontline staff to managers is a common defence, allowing workers to sidestep the anxiety of decision-making, while radically eroding their sense of autonomy, discretion and scope for professional judgement. Andrew Whittaker's (2011) paper in which he discusses a 'practice near' ethnographic study of four frontline child protection teams is a very helpful introduction to this way of thinking but, as discussed above, see also Lees (2014) and Cooper and Lees (2014) for accounts that offer insight into the challenges that modern organisational cultures pose for child protection practitioners in realising their potential as autonomous professionals.

At the 'frontline'

I wish to pause to think about the language we deploy in discussing child protection work. The 'frontline', 'bombardment', 'siege mentality' and many other common metaphors speak to an underlying sense of this work as akin to war, as Beckett (2003) has noted. But we should surely be reflective and questioning about our discourses; otherwise they inhabit us, and we them, in an uncritical way and this constrains our capacity for 'agency', our ability to take more charge of the work and our experience of it, rather than it controlling us. Child protection work may sometimes seem as if it is a warzone, but it is not war. To forget this is to forget that its aim is ultimately benign and reparative – to protect children and help struggling parents and carers with the most important 'task' any of us assume in our lives.

I wish to comment on an extract drawn from a research interview, part of a doctoral project for which I am the supervisor (Noyes unpublished) that aims to record the emotional realities of frontline workers' experiences and states of mind. By way of background, the very experienced social worker, who is the respondent in the research interview, describes in her own words what it is like to work with a young mother of a two-year-old child on a child protection plan for 18 months or so. The worker's name (Kate) has been changed for purposes of confidentiality. I suggest this research interview excerpt shows the vividness of language that the practitioner searches for in order to convey to the research interviewer how she has experienced elements of her contact with the mother. I would also like to draw attention to the importance of a receptive, listening *supervisory-type* presence to allow the worker to communicate their experience.

Case excerpt

Interviewer: And you're doing a kind of sucking motion with your mouth…

Social worker (SW): Yes well […] she sort of sucks the life out of you and I [laughs] have to go, and just getting her to sort of […]it has been a struggle. I've worked with her now […] for 18 months, just over 18 months and […] there have been visits when I have been talking about really serious concerns around relationships with her partner and issues around the child protection plan […] and I just think 'Am I getting through to you?' How am I communicating with you?' But I go away thinking…I get in the car and I go […] oh […]

Interviewer: And you're bodily showing me that you sag.

SW: Yes, [raises voice] I do sag and I just think, 'oh goodness me', and I sort of go ooh […] do that with my head, sort of shaking my head, and I just think, 'Did I get through to her at all?' And as I say, it can be really difficult things or it can be really positive things I'm going with, and I still can get the same response. It did very much feel like I was talking to myself over and over and saying the same thing. That's quite disheartening going every visit, sometimes two, three times a week when it's really serious and saying the same thing over and over again but [hits table/chair] reflecting back I think well, actually all that hard work you put in with her, Kate, has paid off because some of it must have soaked in because she's changed slowly but surely maybe at her own pace but she has actually made progress really but […] and I like her, I do like her, I've got a lot of empathy and sympathy for her. You know, I feel quite sorry for her because […] with her experiences and her child […] and I think she wants to be nurtured by me as well and sort of give her the positives and nurture and that's been a resistance in me because I'm *not* her mum and um don't want to be put into the mum role – it's a sort of carrot and stick with her all the time.

What can we notice about this social worker's narration of her experience in the context of a research interview? There is a whole dimension of the worker's communications to the researcher that is not just non-verbal, but actively expressed through bodily gestures – sighs, sagging, sucking, hitting the table. The researcher can be seen, in the interview transcript, reflecting back to the worker her impressions of the worker's body language as she, the worker, recounts experiences of working with this young mother. What I see in this research interview is an example of the components of receptive, listening *supervisory-type* presence.

My further observation of this account within the research transcript is that whole areas of the young woman's emotional experience cannot be communicated in a way that the worker can fully understand or fully make sense of. The language used and her actions suggest to me a worker who is stuck – a case that is emotionally stuck, despite the fact that there is engagement between the mother and the worker and some progress described in the case. The sense of 'banging one's head against a brick wall' is not just spoken about but conveyed in the narration itself – the emphatic repetition of *serious*, the *same*, *every*, *nothing* perhaps impacts on the listener to produce the same effect the young woman has had on the worker – a kind of deadening of the relationship maybe.

The worker is aware of being drawn into a 'mothering' role, despite herself; such is the power of the essentially unconscious communications to which she is subject. It seems the young mother cannot really talk *about* certain aspects of her own experience, especially of her childhood and parenting, but I would suggest they are re-enacted with the worker. These unconscious communications take root in the worker as bodily experiences that are weighing her down. I think the research interviewer does a simple but skilled job of mirroring these unconscious processes back to the worker.

Final observation

In an important paper, mentioned earlier, the American social worker and therapist Selma Fraiberg (Fraiberg *et al.* 1975) evoked the idea of 'ghosts in the nursery', the emotionally active residues of parents' own difficult childhood experiences that are revisited on their children in turn. Ghosts in the nursery are a universal experience, as Fraiberg *et al.* make plain, but in certain cases cannot be laid to rest. In such cases, the child protection worker becomes the latest recipient of a visitation from these 'ghosts', who take up residence in the workers' bodies and minds in disturbing, perplexing and burdensome ways. But this can only happen if the worker is first of all available to create a relationship in which this can happen. This is step one; step two is about making sense of these communications with the help of others; and finally, step three is the skill of making use of new understanding about family relationships to start a process of change in these relationships. Sometimes this is not possible even with specialised therapeutic input, and then begins the difficult task of assessing whether the right course of action in the child's long-term interests may be removal.

This brings us more or less full circle, to some of the core dilemmas of child protection work outlined at the start of the chapter. The weight of the world cannot always be allowed to remain with the child, and so it passes to us as members of the child protection system to assume responsibility for it, as best we can.

Contributor Profiles

Fiona Arney is the Chair of Child Protection and Director of the Australian Centre for Child Protection at the University of South Australia, Adelaide and the Chair of the South Australian Council for the Care of Children. She has two decades of experience in research with vulnerable children and their families, and the organisations and systems that support them. She works closely with governments, service providers and communities to find, implement and evaluate innovative policy and practice solutions to help children and their families to thrive. She is particularly interested in the prevention of child abuse and neglect, and in alternative approaches to child protection for Indigenous families.

Leah Bromfield is Deputy Director of the Australian Centre for Child Protection at the University of South Australia, Adelaide. She joined the Centre in 2010 after six years as a senior research fellow at the Australian Institute of Family Studies' National Child Protection Clearinghouse. She is a well-regarded research expert in issues affecting child protection systems, chronic maltreatment and cumulative harm, and research to practice. She has worked closely with government on establishing and implementing child-welfare reforms.

Andrew Cooper is Professor of Social Work at The Tavistock Centre in London, England, UK and at the University of East London. He has written extensively on the importance of relationship-based and therapeutic social work practice, especially in child protection work. He has participated in, and published, many papers and books about a long series of cross-national European research studies into child protection practices and systems that reveal the possibilities for alternative approaches to the dominant British model.

Brigid Daniel is Professor of Social Work at the School of Applied Social Science at the University of Stirling, Scotland, UK. Her research and publications are in the fields of child neglect, children's resilience and professional responses aimed at the protection of children and at the promotion of their wellbeing.

Tim Dare is Head of Philosophy at the University of Auckland, New Zealand. He is also a lawyer and former research clerk to the New Zealand High Court. He is the author of *The Counsel of Rogues? A Defence of the Standard Conception of the Lawyer's Role* (published by Ashgate, 2009), co-editor of *Professional Ethics and Personal Integrity* (published by Cambridge Scholars Publishing, 2010), and the author of many articles and book chapters on the philosophy of law and applied and professional ethics, including pieces on vaccination, parental rights to consent to their children's medical treatment, and oncologists' views about giving information about unfunded treatments beyond the means of their patients. He was part of a team that produced a computerised risk assessment tool for child maltreatment, which is a central part of the New Zealand Government's White Paper for Vulnerable Children.

Melissa O'Donnell is a Psychologist and National Health and Medical Research Fellow at the Telethon Kids Institute, The University of Western Australia, Perth. She utilises linked government data from the Western Australian Departments of Health, Child Protection, Education, Corrective Services and Disability Services to investigate outcomes and risk and protective factors for children who have experienced abuse and neglect. She also collaborates with government agencies to inform policy-relevant research and to translate findings to improve outcomes of children through prevention and early intervention.

Jason Hart is Senior Lecturer in the Anthropology of Development, University of Bath, England, UK and Research Associate at the Refugee Studies Centre, University of Oxford, UK. Much of his work has explored the experience of young people on the margins of society and the global economy, relating these to the values, assumptions and approaches of agencies making interventions. Aside from his academic research he has been employed as a consultant author, evaluator and trainer by various United Nations (UN) and non-governmental organisations. He has also served as an advisor to the UN in the formulation of studies, guidelines and policies.

Walter Lorenz has been Professor for Applied Social Science at the Free University of Bozen-Bolzano in Northern Italy since 2001; he coordinates a professional social work programme and has been Principal of the same university since 2008. A native of Germany, he qualified as a social worker at the London School of Economics, UK, and practised this profession in East London before taking up a teaching position at University College, Cork, Ireland in 1978 where he became Jean Monnet Professor in 1995. His research interests include intercultural pedagogy, social pedagogy, comparative aspects of social work and social policy in Europe, and quality standards in social services.

Stewart McDougall is a Research Assistant at the Australian Centre for Child Protection at the University of South Australia, Adelaide. His research interests include the intersection of prenatal exposure to alcohol and child maltreatment, the fathering practices of violent men, and the executive functioning of children who experience maltreatment.

Janice McGhee is Senior Lecturer in Social Work in the School of Social and Political Science, The University of Edinburgh. Her research interests lie in child care policy and law including the Scottish children's hearings system and child protection. Currently she leads the social work strand of the Administrative Data Research Centre – Scotland, part of an ESRC funded UK-wide administrative data research network.

Heather Montgomery is a Reader in the Anthropology of Childhood at The Open University, Milton Keynes, England, UK. A social anthropologist by background, she wrote her PhD on child prostitution in Thailand and now works on the ethnography and theory of childhood within anthropology. She is the author of *Modern Babylon? Prostituting children in Thailand* (published by Bergmann, 2001), *An Introduction to Childhood. Anthropological perspectives on children's lives* (published by Wiley-Blackwell, 2009) and the editor of *Global Childhood, Local Issues* (published by Policy Press, 2013).

Tarja Pösö is Professor in Social Work at the School of Social Sciences and Humanities, University of Tampere, Finland. She has longstanding experience in studying child welfare from different perspectives and has a keen interest in cross-cultural perspectives and exploring methods and ethics for child welfare studies. Her work has been published in national and international journals and books.

Trevor Spratt is the Director of the Children's Research Centre at Trinity College Dublin, Ireland. He has worked for ten years in social work practice with children and families. His research interests are decision-making by professionals, how policy objectives are translated into professional practices, the development of child protection systems internationally and the impact of early adversities in childhood as realised across the life-course. His first academic position was with the University of Ulster, Northern Ireland, UK in 1997, moving thereafter to Queen's University Belfast, Northern Ireland, UK in 2000 before taking up his current post in 2014.

E. Kay M. Tisdall is Professor of Childhood Policy and Co-Director of the Centre for Research on Families and Relationships (CRFR), at The University of Edinburgh, Scotland, UK. She established the MSc in Childhood Studies at the University of Edinburgh, which is underlined by the UN Convention on the Rights of the Child and specialises in research skills training in directly engaging with children and young people. She has an extensive policy and academic interest in children and young people's rights and participation, with collaborative projects funded by the Leverhulme Trust and the UK's Economic and Social Research Council and ensuing publications in journals, chapters and books (e.g. *Children and Young People's Participation and its Transformative Potential: Learning from across Countries* (2014, London: Palgrave Macmillan)).

Lorraine Waterhouse is Professor (emerita) of Social Work in the School of Social and Political Science, The University of Edinburgh. Her longstanding research interest is in child care and child protection. She is currently working on the position of child-welfare involved mothers in social services from a cross-disciplinary perspective.

References

Abu-Sada, C. (ed.) (2012) *Dilemmas, Challenges, and Ethics of Humanitarian Action: Reflections on Medecins Sans Frontières Perception Project.* London: McGill-Queen's University Press.

Action for Children (2014) *Children and the Benefit Cap.* London: Action for Children.

Adorno, T. (1963) *Problems of Moral Philosophy* (trans. R. Livingstone). Stanford: Stanford University Press.

Agamben, G. (1995) *Homo Sacer Sovereign Power and Bare Life.* Stanford: Stanford University Press.

Ager, A., Boothby, N. and Bremer, M. (2008) 'Using the "protective environment" framework to analyse children's protection needs in Darfur.' *Disasters 33,* 4, 548–573.

Alderson, P. (2012) 'Young children's human rights: A sociological analysis.' *International Journal of Children's Rights 20,* 177–198.

Allen, G. (2011) *Early Intervention: The Next Steps.* London: Cabinet Office.

Anda, R., Butchart, A., Felitti, V. and Brown, D. (2010) 'Building a framework for global surveillance of the public health implications of adverse childhood experiences.' *American Journal of Preventative Medicine 39,* 1, 93–98.

Anderson, J. and Honneth, A. (2005) 'Autonomy, Vulnerability, Recognition and Justice.' In J. Christman and J. Anderson (eds) *Autonomy and the Challenges to Liberalism: New Essays.* New York, NY: Cambridge University Press.

Aptekar, L. and Stoecklin, D. (2014) *Street Children and Homeless Youth: A Cross-cultural Perspective.* Dordrecht: Springer.

Arendt, H. (1958) *The Human Condition.* Chicago, IL: University of Chicago Press.

Arneil, B. (2002) 'Becoming versus Being: A Critical Analysis of the Child in Liberal Theory.' In D. Archard and C. M. Macleod (eds) *The Moral and Political Status of Children.* Oxford: Oxford University Press.

Arney, F., Lange, R. and Zufferey, C. (2010) 'Responding to Parents with Complex Needs Who Come into Contact With Child Protection Services.' In F. Arney and D. Scott (eds) *Working with Vulnerable Families: A Partnership Approach.* Melbourne: Cambridge University Press.

Arney, F., McGuinness, K. and Westby, M. (2012) *Report on the Implementation of Family Group Conferencing with Aboriginal Families in Alice Springs.* Darwin: Menzies School of Health Research.

Arnold, L., Maio-Taddeo, C., Scott, D. and Zufferey, C. (2008) *Professionals Protecting Children: Child Protection and Social Work Education in Australia.* Adelaide: Australian Centre for Child Protection.

Australian Institute of Health and Welfare (2014) *Indigenous Child Safety.* Canberra: Australian Government.

Bacon, R. (1988) 'Countertransference in a Case Conference: Resistance and Rejection in Work with Abusing Families and their Children. In G. Pearson, J. Treseder and M. Yelloly (eds) *Social Work and the Legacy of Freud.* Basingstoke: Macmillan.

Bardy, M. and Heino, T. (2013) 'Katsaus Lastensuojelun Toimintaympäristöihin: Paniikista Toivoon Ja Näköalat Auki [An Overview of the Contexts of Child Welfare: From Panic to Hope].' In M. Bardy (ed.) *Lastensuojelun Ytimissä [In the Core of Child Welfare]*. Helsinki: THL.

Barlow, J. and Scott, J. (2010) *Safeguarding in the 21st Century: Where to Now?* Totnes: Research in Practice.

Baumberg, B., Bell, K., Gaffney, D., Deacon, R., Hood, C. and Sage, D. (2012) *Benefits Stigma in Britain.* London: Elizabeth Finn Care, University of Kent.

Baumrind, D. (1972) 'Socialization and Instrumental Competence in Young Children.' In W. W. Hartup (ed.) *The Young Child: Reviews of Research, Vol. 2.* Washington, DC: National Association for the Education of Young Children.

BBC (1999) 'Child soldiers in Sri Lanka.' *BBC News.* Available at http://news.bbc.co.uk/1/hi/world/south_asia/252861.stm, accessed 24 March 2015.

Beah, I. (2007) *A Long Way Gone: The True Story of a Child Soldier.* London: Harper Perennial.

Beatty, C. and Fothergill, S. (2013) *Hitting the Poorest Places the Hardest: The Local and Regional Impact of Welfare Reform.* Sheffield: Sheffield Hallam University.

Beckett, C. (2003) 'The language of siege: military metaphors in the spoken language of social work.' *British Journal of Social Work 33*, 5, 625–639.

Beinin, J. (2007) 'Letter from al-Tuwani.' *MERIP 244.* Available at www.merip.org/mer/mer244/beinin_tuwani.html, accessed 24 March 2015.

Bessell, S. and Gal, T. (2009) 'Forming partnerships: the human rights of children in need of care and protection.' *International Journal of Children's Rights 17*, 283–298.

Beyondblue and Perinatal Mental Health Consortium (2008) *Perinatal Mental Health National Action Plan 2008–2010: Full Report.* Melbourne: Beyondblue.

Biestek, F. P. (1957) *The Casework Relationship.* Chicago, IL: Loyola University Press.

Biggeri, M., Ballet, J. and Comim, F. (2011) *Children and the Capability Approach.* Basingstoke/New York, NY: Palgrave Macmillan.

Bissell, S. (2011) *Introduction to Child Protection in Emergencies.* Lecture given at Columbia University, 10 March 2011. Available at http://childprotection.wikischolars.columbia.edu/Session+1, accessed 24 March 2015.

Bissell, S. (2012) 'The "State of the Art" in Child Protection Systems: Keynote Address.' *A Better Way to Protect All Children: Child Protection Systems Conference* New Delhi. Available at https://knowledge-gateway.org/sharekluo5tgnjrn31p71ra1zp7b2hnkl48j5vz27/childprotection/cpsystems/cpsconference/library, accessed 24 March 2015.

Blacklock, S., Bonser, G., Hayden, P. and Menzies, K. (2013) 'Kinship care: embracing a new practice paradigm.' *Developing Practice 35*, Winter.

Blair, T. (2006) *Our Sovereign Value: Fairness.* Speech given to the Rowntree Foundation, York, 5 September 2006. Available at Available at www.britishpoliticalspeech.org/speech-archive.htm?speech=283, accessed 30 April 2015

Bledsoe, C. (1990) 'No success without struggle: social mobility and hardship for foster children in Sierra Leone.' *Man (N.S.) 25*, 1, 70–88.

Boddy, J., Statham, J., McQuail, S., Petrie, P. and Owen, C. (2009) *Working at the 'Edges' of Care? European Models of Support for Young People and Families.* London: Department for Children, Schools and Families and Thomas Coram Research Unit, Institute of Education.

Bonvin, J. M. and Stoecklin, D. (2014) 'Introduction.' In D. Stoecklin and J.-M. Bonvin (eds) *Children's Rights and the Capability Approach: Challenges and Prospects.* Dordrecht: Springer.

Bower, M. (2005) 'Families Who See Help as the Problem.' In M. Bower (ed.) Psychoanalytic Theory for Social Work Practice: Thinking Under Fire. Abingdon: Routledge.

Bourdieu, P. (1999) *The Weight of the World.* Cambridge: Polity Press.

Bowlby, J. (1977) 'The making and breaking of affectional bonds.' *The British Journal of Psychiatry 130*, 201–210.

Bowlby, J. (1985) 'Violence in the family as a function of the attachment system.' *American Journal of Psychoanalysis 44*, 9–27.

Bradley, J. and Rustin, M. (eds) (2008) *Work Discussion: Learning from Reflective Practice in Work with Children and Families*. London. Karnac (Tavistock Clinic Series).

Brandon, M., Bailey, S., Belderson, P. and Larsson, B. (2013) *Neglect and Serious Case Reviews: A Report from the University of East Anglia Commissioned by NSPCC*. Norwich: University of East Anglia/NSPCC.

Brandon, M., Bailey, S., Belderson, P., Warren, C., Gardner, R. and Dodsworth, J. (2009) *Understanding Serious Case Reviews and their Impact*. London: Department for Children, Schools and Families.

Brandon, M., Belderson, P., Warren, C., Howe, D. *et al*. (2008) *Analysing Child Deaths and Serious Injury through Abuse and Neglect: What Can We Learn? A Biennial Analysis of Serious Case Reviews 2003–05*. London, Department of Children, Schools and Families.

Brandon, M., Sidebotham, P., Bailey, S., Belderson, P. *et al*. (2012), *New Learning from Serious Case Reviews: A Two Year Report for 2009–2011*. London: Department for Education.

Briggs, C., Ryan, D., Brown, N., Gray, J. *et al*. (2010) *Professionals Protecting Children: Child Protection and Nursing and Midwifery Education Curriculum Standards*. Adelaide: University of Technology Sydney and the Australian Centre for Child Protection.

Broadhurst, K., Hall, C., Wastell, D., White, S. and Pithouse, A. (2010) 'Risk, instrumentalism and the humane project in social work: Identifying the informal logics of risk management in children's statutory services.' *British Journal of Social Work 40*, 1046–1064

Bromfield, L. and Arney, F. (2008) 'Developing a road map for research: Identifying priorities for a national child protection research agenda.' *Child Abuse Prevention Issues 28*.

Bromfield, L. and Osborn, A. (2007) 'Getting the big picture: A synopsis and critique of Australian out-of-home care research.' *Child Abuse Prevention Issues 26*.

Bromfield, L., Gillingham, P. and Higgins, D. (2007) 'Cumulative harm and chronic child maltreatment.' *Developing Practice 19*, 34–42.

Bromfield, L., Lamont, A., Parker, R. and Horsfall, B. (2010) 'Issues for the safety and wellbeing of children in families with multiple and complex problems: The co-occurence of domestic violence, parental substance misuse, and mental health problems.' *National Child Protection Clearinghouse 33*.

Brown, D. J. (2006) 'Working the system: re-thinking the institutionally organized role of mothers and the reduction of "risk" in Child Protection Work.' *Social Problems 53*, 3, 352–370.

Brown, K. (2011) '"Vulnerability": Handle with care.' *Ethics and Social Welfare 5*, 3, 313–321.

Browne, K. and Chou, S. (n.d.) *A Literature Review on Systems For Early Prediction and Risk Detection In Child Protection in Europe*. Munich: Deutsches Jugendinstitut. Available at www.dji.de/bibs/Expertise_Browne.pdf, accessed 24 March 2015.

Brownell, M. D. and Jutte, D. P. (2013) 'Administrative data linkage as a tool for child maltreatment research.' *Child Abuse and Neglect 37*, 120–124.

Buckley, H. 2005. 'Neglect: No Monopoly on Expertise.' In J. Taylor and B. Daniel (eds) *Child Neglect: Practice Issues for Health and Social Care*. London: Jessica Kingsley Publishers.

Burgess, C., Daniel, B., Scott, J., Dobbin, H., Mulley, K. and Whitfield, E. (2014) *Preventing Child Neglect in the UK: What Makes Services Accessible to Children and Families?* London: Action for Children with University of Stirling.

Burgess, C., Daniel, B., Scott, J., Mulley, K., Derbyshire, D. and Downie, M (2012) *Child Neglect in 2011: An Annual Review by Action for Children in Partnership with the University of Stirling*. London: Action for Children with University of Stirling.

Burgess, C., Daniel, B., Whitfield, E., Derbyshire, D. and Taylor, J. (2013) *Action on Neglect: A Resource Pack*. Stirling: Stirling University with Action for Children.

Burman, E. (1996) 'Local, global or globalized? Child development and international children's rights legislation.' *Childhood 3*, 1, 45–66.

Burton, S. (2009) *The Oversight and Review of Cases in the Light of Changing Circumstances and New Information: How Do People Respond to New (and Challenging) Information?* London: C4EO.

Butchart, A., Phinney Harvey, A., Mian, M., Furniss, T. and Kahane, T. (2006) *Preventing Child Maltreatment: A Guide to Taking Action and Generating Evidence.* Geneva: World Health Organization.

Butler, J. (2005) *Giving an Account of Onseself.* New York, NY: Fordham University Press.

Butrym, S. (1976) *The Nature of Social Work.* Macmillan, London.

Bywaters, P. (2013) 'Inequalities in child welfare: Towards a new policy, research and action agenda.' *British Journal of Social Work* [online] DOI 10.1093/bjsw/bct079.

Cameron, C. (2013) 'Cross-national understandings of the purpose of professional–child relationships: towards a social pedagogical approach.' *International Journal of Social Pedagogy 2,* 1, 3–16.

Carmody, T. (2013) *Queensland Child Protection Commission of Inquiry: Taking Responsibility: A Roadmap for Queensland Child Protection.* Brisbane: Queensland Child Protection Commission of Inquiry.

Cashmore, J. (2011) 'Children's participation in family law decision-making: Theoretical approaches to understanding children's views.' *Children and Youth Services Review 33,* 4, 515–520.

Cashmore, J. and Ainsworth, F. (2004) Audit of Australian Out-of-Home Care research. Sydney: Association of Children's Welfare Agencies.

Cashmore, J., Higgins, D., Bromfield, L. and Scott, D. (2006) 'Recent Australian child protection and out-of-home-care research: What's been done – and what needs to be done?' *Children Australia 31,* 2, 4–11.

Cater, Å. and Øverlien, C. (2014) 'Children exposed to domestic violence: a discussion about research ethics and researchers' responsibilities.' *Nordic Social Work Research* [online] DOI 10.1080/2156857X.2013.801878.

Cavarero, A. (2000) *Relating Narratives: Storytelling and Selfhood* (trans. P. A. Cottman). London: Routledge.

Cawson, P., Wattam, C., Booker, S. and Kelly, G. (2000) *Child Maltreatment in the United Kingdom: A Study of the Prevalence of Child Abuse and Neglect.* London: NSPCC.

Centre on the Developing Child at Harvard University (2010) *The Foundations of Life-long Health Are Built in Early Childhood.* Cambridge, MA: Centre on the Developing Child at Harvard University. Available at www.developingchild.harvard.edu, accessed 24 March 2015.

Center for Reviews and Dissemination (2007) *Review Methods and Resources.* York: University of York.

Child Protection Working Group (2013) *Minimum Standards for Child Protection in Humanitarian Action.* Geneva: Child Protection Working Group. Available at http://cpwg.net/minimum-standards, accessed 24 March 2015.

Children's Improvement Board (2012) *Progress in Implementing The Munro Review of Child Protection and Social Work Reform: A View from The Children's Improvement Board.* London: Children's Improvement Board.

Cleaver, H., Unell, I. and Aldgate, J. (2011) *Children's Needs: Parenting Capacity. Child Abuse: Parental Mental Illness, Learning Disability, Substance Misuse and Domestic Violence* (2nd edition). London: The Stationery Office.

Cooper, A. (2005) 'Surface and depth in the Victoria Climbié Report.' *Child and Family Social Work 10,* 1–9.

Cooper, A. (2014) 'A short psychosocial history of British child abuse and protection: Case studies of problems of mourning in the public sphere.' *Journal of Social Work Practice 28,* 3, 271–285.

Cooper, A. and Lees, A. (2014) 'Spotlit: Defences Against Anxiety in Contemporary Human Service Organisations.' In D. Armstrong and M. Rustin (eds) *Social Defences Against Anxiety: Explorations in the Paradigm.* London: Karnac (Tavistock Clinic Series).

Cooper, A. and Lousada, J. (2005) *Borderline Welfare: Feeling and Fear of Feeling in Modern Welfare.* London: Karnac Books.

Cooper, A. and Whittaker, A. (2014) 'History as tragedy, never as farce: Tracing the long cultural narrative of child protection in England.' *Journal of Social Work Practice 28*, 3, 251–266.

Cornock, M. and Montgomery, H. (2011) 'Children's rights in and out of the womb.' *International Journal of Children's Rights 19*, 3–19.

Cornwall, A. and Nyamu-Musembi, C. (2004) 'Putting the "rights-based approach" to development into perspective.' *Third World Quarterly 25*, 8, 1415–1437.

Cott, J. (2013) *Susan Sontag: The Complete Rolling Stone Interview.* Newhaven, CT and London: Yale University Press.

Council of Australian Governments (2009) *Protecting Children is Everyone's Business: The National Framework for Protecting Australia's Children 2009–2020.* Canberra: Commonwealth of Australia.

Cronin, D. (2010) *Europe's Alliance with Israel: Aiding the Occupation.* London: Pluto Press.

Dalziel, K. and Segal, L. (2012) 'Home visiting programmes for the prevention of child maltreatment: cost effectiveness of 33 programmes.' *Archives of Disease in Childhood 97*, 9, 787–798.

Daniel, B. (1998) 'A picture of powerlessness: an exploration of child neglect and ways in which social workers and parents can be empowered towards efficacy.' *International Journal of Child and Family Welfare 3*, 3, 269–285.

Daniel, B. (2010) 'Concepts of adversity, risk, vulnerability and resilience: A discussion in the context of the "child protection system".' *Social Policy and Society 9*, 2, 231–241.

Daniel, B., Burgess, C. and Scott, J. (2012) *Review of Child Neglect in Scotland.* Edinburgh: Scottish Government.

Daniel, B., Burgess, C., Scott, J. and Mulley, K (2013a) *The State of Child Neglect in the UK.* London: Action for Children with University of Stirling.

Daniel, B., Burgess, C., Scott, J., Mulley, K. and Dobbin, H. (2013b) *The State of Child Neglect in the UK: An Annual Review by Action for Children in Partnership with the University of Stirling.* London: Action for Children with University of Stirling.

Daniel, B., Taylor, J. and Scott, J. (2009a) *Noticing and Helping the Neglected Child: A Review of the Literature: Final Report to the DfE and DoH.* Stirling: University of Stirling.

Daniel, B., Taylor, J. and Scott, J. (2009b) 'Recognition of neglect and early response: Summary of a systematic literature review.' *International Journal of Child and Family Welfare 12*, 4, 120–33.

Daniel, B., Taylor, J. and Scott, J. (2010) 'Recognition of neglect and early response: Overview of a systematic review of the literature.' *Child and Family Social Work 15*, 2, 248–57.

Darlington, Y. and Feeney, J. (2008) 'Collaboration between mental health and child protection services: Professionals' perceptions of best practice.' *Children and Youth Services Review 30*, 2, 187–198.

Davidson, G., Devaney, J. and Spratt, T. (2010) 'The impact of adversity in childhood on outcomes in adulthood: Research lessons and limitations.' *Journal of Social Work 10*, 4, 369–390.

Davies, C. and Ward, H. (2011) *Safeguarding Children Across Services: Messages From Research on Identifying and Responding to Child Maltreatment.* London: Department for Education.

Dawe, S. and Harnett, P. H. (2013a) 'Working with Parents with Substance Misuse Problems: a Parents under Pressure Perspective.' In F. Arney and D. Scott (eds) *Working with Vulnerable Families: A Partnership Approach.* Melbourne: Cambridge University Press.

Dawe, S. and Harnett, P. H. (2013b) *Submission to the Queensland Child Protection Commission of Inquiry.* Nathan: Griffith University.

Delfabbro, P., Fernandez, E., McCormick, J. and Kettler, L. (2014) 'An analysis of reunification from out-of-home care in three Australian states.' *Child Indicators Research* [online] DOI 10.1007/ s12187-014-9238-6.

Delfabbro, P., Hirte, C., Rogers, N. and Wilson, R. (2010a) 'The over-representation of young Aboriginal or Torres Strait Islander people in the South Australian child system: A longitudinal analysis.' *Children and Youth Services Review 32*, 10, 1418–1425.

Delfabbro, P., Hirte, C., Wilson, R. and Rogers, N. (2010b) 'Longitudinal trends in child protection statistics in South Australia: A study of unit record data.' *Children Australia 35*, 3, 4–10.

Delfabbro, P., King, D. and Barber, J. (2010) 'Children in foster care: Five years on.' *Children Australia 35*, 1, 22–30.

Department for Education and Skills (2004) *Every Child Matters.* London: The Stationery Office.

Department of Families Housing Community Services and Indigenous Affairs together with the National Framework Implementation Working Group (2011) *National Research Agenda for Protecting Children: 2011–2014.* Canberra: Commonwealth of Australia.

Department of Health (1995) *Child Protection: Messages From Research.* London: Department of Health.

Devaney, J. (2004) 'Relating outcomes to objectives in child protection.' *Child and Family Social Work 9*, 27–38.

Devaney, J. (2009) 'Chronic child abuse: the characteristics and careers of children caught in the child protection system.' *British Journal of Social Work 39*, 1, 24–45.

Devaney, J., Bunting, L., Hayes, D. and Lazenbatt, A. (2013) *Translating Learning into Action: An Overview of Key Learning from Case Management Reviews 2003–2008.* Belfast: DHSSPS.

Dickison, M. (2013) 'Beneficiaries "attacked on all sides".' *The New Zealand Herald*, 6 February, A3.

Dixon, R. and Nussbaum, M. (2012) 'Children's rights and a capability approach: The question of special priority.' *Cornell Law Review 97*, Public Law Working Paper No. 384.

Doll, R. and Hill, A. B. (1950) 'Smoking and carcinoma of the lung.' *British Medical Journal 2*, 4682, 739–748.

Douglas, M. (1966) *Purity and Danger: An Analysis of Concepts of Pollution and Taboo.* London: Routledge.

Dworkin, R. (1977) *Taking Rights Seriously.* Boston, MA: Harvard University Press.

Ebrahim, A. (2003) 'Accountability In practice: mechanisms for NGOs.' *World Development 31*, 5, 813–829.

Egeland, B. (1991) 'A Longitudinal Study of High Risk Families: Issues and Findings.' In R. H. Starr and D. A. Wolfe (eds) *The Effects of Child Abuse and Neglect: Issues and Research.* New York, NY: Guilford Press.

Egeland, B., Sroufe, L. A. and Erickson, M. (1983) 'The developmental consequences of different patterns of maltreatment.' *Child Abuse and Neglect 7*, 459–469.

Ellonen, N. (2012) *Kurinalaiset: Lasten ja Vanhempien Välisten Ristiriitojen Ratkaiseminen Perheessä [Solving the Domestic Conflicts Between Parents and Children.]* Tampere: Poliisiammattikorkeakoulu.

Ellonen, N. and Pösö, T. (2011) 'Violence experiences in care: some methodological remarks based on the Finnish Child Victim survey.' *Child Abuse Review 20*, 3, 197–212.

Ellonen, N., Kääriäinen, J., Salmi, V. and Sariola, H. (2008) *Lapset ja Nuoret Väkivallan Uhreina [Children and Adolescents as Victims of Violence].* Helsinki: Police College of Finland and National Research Institute for Legal Policy.

Ellonen, N. and Pösö, T. (2014) 'Hesitation as a system response to children exposed to violence.' *International Journal of Children's Rights 22*, 4, 730–747.

Ennew, J. (1995) 'Outside Childhood: Street Children's Rights.' In B. Franklin (ed.) *The Handbook of Children's Rights.* London: Routledge.

Ennew, J. (1998) *The African Contexts of Children's Rights: Seminar Report.* Harare: CODESRIA.

Eriksson, M. (2012) 'Participation for children exposed to domestic violence? Social workers' approaches and children's strategies.' *European Journal of Social Work 15*, 2, 205–221.

Eskonen, I. (2005) *Perheväkivalta Lasten Kertomana [Domestic Violence Narrated by Children].* Tampere: Tampere University Press.

Fallon, B., Trocmé, N., Fluke, J., MacLaurin, B., Tonmyr, L. and Yuan, Y. Y. (2010) 'Methodological challenges in measuring child maltreatment.' *Child Abuse and Neglect 34*, 1, 70–79.

Family and Parenting Institute (2012) *The Family Report Card 2012*. London: Family and Parenting Institute.

Farmer, E. and Lutman, E. (2009) *Case Management and Outcomes for Neglected Children Returned to their Parents: A Five Year Follow-up Study (Research Brief)*. London: Department of Children, Schools and Families.

Farmer, E., Sturgess, W. and O'Neill, T. (2008) *Reunification of Looked After Children with their Parents: Patterns, Interventions and Outcomes: Research Brief*. London: DCSF.

Farmer, E., Sturgess, W., O'Neill, T. and Wijedasa, D. (2011) *Achieving Successful Returns from Care: What Makes Reunification Work?* London: BAAF.

Featherstone, B. (1999) 'Taking mothering seriously: the implications for child protection.' *Child and Family Social Work 4*, 43–53.

Featherstone, B., White, S. and Morris, K. (2014) *Re-imagining Child Protection*. Bristol: Policy Press.

Fergusson, D. M., Horwood, L. J. and Woodward, L. J. (2000) 'The stability of child abuse reports: a longitudinal study of the reporting behaviour of young adults.' *Psychological Medicine 30*, 3, 529–544.

Fineman, M. A. (2008) 'The vulnerable subject: Anchoring equality in the human condition.' *Yale Journal of Law and Feminism 20*, 1, 1–18.

Fineman, M. A. (2010/2011) 'The vulnerable subject and the responsive state.' *Emory Law Journal 60*, 251–275.

Forder, A. (1966) *Social Casework and Administration*. London: Faber and Faber.

Forman, S., Olin, S. S., Hoagwood, K., Crowe, M. and Saka, N. (2009) 'Evidence-based interventions in schools: Developers' views of implementation barriers and facilitators.' *School Mental Health 1*, 1, 26–36.

Forrester, D., Kershaw, S., Moss, H. and Hughes, L. (2008) 'Communication skills in child protection: How do social workers talk to parents?' *Child and Family Social Work 13*, 1, 41–51.

Forrester, D., Westlake, D. and Glynn, G. (2012) 'Parental resistance and social worker skills: Towards a theory of motivational social work.' *Child and Family Social Work 17*, 2, 118–129.

Forsberg, H. (2005) '"Talking Feels Like You Wouldn't Love Dad Anymore": Children's Emotions, Close Relations and Domestic Violence.' In M. Eriksson, Maria, M. Hester, S. Keskinen and K. Pringle (eds) *Tackling Men's Violence in Families: Nordic Issues and Dilemmas*. Bristol: Policy Press.

Forsberg, H. and Pösö, T. (2008) 'Ambiguous position of the child in supervised meetings.' *Child and Family Social Work 13*, 1, 52–60.

Fraiberg, S., Adelson, E. and Shapiro, V. (1975) 'Ghosts in the nursery: a psychoanalytic approach to the problems of impaired mother-infant relationships.' *Journal of the American Academy of Child Psychiatry 14*, 3, 387–421

Frank, A. (1947/2007) *The Diary of a Young Girl*. London: Puffin Classics.

Freeman, M. D. A. (1983) *The Rights and Wrongs of Children*. London: Francis Pinter.

Freisthler, B., Gruenewald, P. J., Remer, L. G., Lery, B. and Needell, B. (2007) 'Exploring the spatial dynamics of alcohol outlets and child protection service referrals, substantiations and foster care entries.' *Child Maltreatment 12*, 2, 114–124.

Frosh, S. (2011) *Feelings*. London: Routledge.

Gibson, C. and Morphett, K. (2011) 'Creative responses to the needs of homeless children: Promising practice.' *Developing Practice 28*, Autumn.

Giddens, A. (1991) *Modernity and Self-Identity: Self and Society in the Late Modern Age*. Cambridge: Polity Press.

Gilbert, N., Parton, N. and Skiveness, M. (2011) *Child Protection Systems: International Trends and Orientations*. New York, NY: OUP.

Gilbert, R., Fluke, J., O'Donnell, M., Gonzalez-Izquierdo, A. *et al.* (2012) 'Child maltreatment: Variation in trends and policies in six developed countries.' *Lancet 379*, 758–772.

Gilbert, R., Kemp, A., Thoburn, J., Sidebotham, P. *et al.* (2009) 'Recognising and responding to child maltreatment.' *Lancet 373*, 9658, 167–180.

Gillingham, P. and Humphreys, C. (2010) 'Child protection practitioners and decision-making tools: Observations and reflections from the front line.' *British Journal of Social Work 40*, 8, 2598–2616.

Goldstein, J., Freud, A. and Solnit, A. J. (1973) *Beyond the Best Interests of the Child.* New York, NY: The Free Press.

Gonzalez-Izquierdo, A., Woodman, J., Copley, L., van der Meulen, J. *et al.* (2010) 'Variation in recording of child maltreatment in administrative records of hospital admissions for injury in England, 1997–2009.' *Archives of Disease in Childhood 95*, 918–925.

Goody, E. (1982) *Parenthood and Social Reproduction: Fostering and Occupational Roles in West Africa.* Cambridge: Cambridge University Press.

Gottlieb, A. (2004) *The Afterlife is Where We Come From: The Culture of Infancy in West Africa.* Chicago, IL: Chicago University Press.

Gottlieb, A. (2014) 'First Acts of Small Violence: Reflections on Breastfeeding and Enemas in West Africa.' In K. Wells, E. Burman, H. Montgomery and A. Watson (eds) *Childhood, Youth and Violence in Global Contexts: Research and Practice in Dialogue.* Basingstoke: Palgrave Macmillan.

Gove, M. (2012) *The Failure of Child Protection and the Need for a Fresh Start.* Speech given to the Institute of Public Policy, 16 November 2012. Available at www.gov.uk/government/speeches/the-failure-of-child-protection-and-the-need-for-a-fresh-start, accessed 24 March 2015.

Guthridge, S., Ryan, P., Condon, J., Bromfield, L., Moss, J. and Lynch, J. (2012) 'Trends in child abuse and neglect among Northern Territory children, 1999 to 2010.' *Medical Journal of Australia 197*, 11, 637–641.

Hämäläinen, U. and Kangas, O. (2010) *Perhepiirissä [Within the Family Circle].* Helsinki: Kelan Tutkimusosasto.

Hamilton, G. (1940) *Theory and Practice of Social Casework.* New York, NY: Columbia University Press.

Harnett, P. H. (2007) 'A procedure for assessing parents capacity for change in child protection cases.' *Children and Youth Services Review 29*, 9, 1179–1188.

Hart, J. (2012) 'The spatialisation of child protection: notes from the occupied Palestinian territory.' *Development in Practice 22*, 4, 473–485.

Hart, J. and Kvittingen, A. (2015) 'Tested at the margins: The contingent rights of displaced Iraqi children in Jordan.' New Issues in Refugee Research 272. Geneva: UNHCR. Available at www.unhcr.org/cgi-bin/texis/vtx/search?page=&comid=4a1d3be46&cid=49aea93a6a&scid=49aea93a3b, accessed 30 April 2015.

Hart, J. and Lo Forte, C. (2010) *Protecting Palestinian Children from Political Violence: The Role of the International Community: Refugee Studies Centre Policy Briefing No. 5.* Oxford: Refugee Studies Centre. Available (in English and Arabic) at www.rsc.ox.ac.uk, accessed 24 March 2015.

Hart, J. and Lo Forte, C. (2013) 'Mandated to fail?: International agencies and the protection of Palestinian children.' *Disasters 37*, 4, 627–645.

Harwin, J., Ryan, M., Tunnard, J., Pokhrel, S. *et al.* (2011) *The Family Drug and Alcohol Court (FDAC) Evaluation Project Final Report.* London: Brunel University.

Hauss, G. (2008) *The Dual Mandate.* Opladen: B. Budrich.

Hayes, D. and Devaney, J. (2004) 'Accessing social work case files for research purposes: some issues and problems.' *Qualitative Social Work 3*, 3, 313–333.

Hayes, D. and Spratt, T. (2009) 'Child welfare interventions: Patterns of social work practice.' *British Journal of Social Work 39*, 8, 1575–1597.

Hayes, D. and Spratt, T. (2014) 'Child welfare as child protection then and now: what social workers did and continue to do.' *British Journal of Social Work 44*, 3, 615–635.

Herring, J. (2012) 'Vulnerability, Children and the Law.' In M. Freeman (ed.) *Law and Childhood Studies.* Oxford: Oxford University Press.

Higgins, D., Adams, R. M., Bromfield, L., Richardson, N. and Aldana, M. S. (2005) *National Audit of Australian Child Protection Research 1995–2004.* Melbourne: Australian Institute of Family Studies.

Hiilamo, H. (2009) 'What could explain the dramatic rise in out-of-home placement in Finland in the 1990s and early 2000s?' *Children and Youth Services Review 31,* 2, 177–184.

Hiitola, J. (2011) 'Vanhempien tekemä väkivalta huostaanottoasiakirjoissa [Violence perpetrated by parents in the documents of out-of-home placements].' *Janus 19,*1, 4–19.

Hill, M., Stafford, A. and Green Lister, P. (2002) 'International Perspectives on Child Protection.' Edinburgh: Scottish Executive (unpublished).

Hindman, H. D. (ed.) (2009) *The World of Child Labor: An Historical and Regional Survey.* New York, NY: M. E. Sharpe.

Hodge, D. R., Lacasse, J. R. and Benson, O. (2012) 'Influential papers in social work discourse: The 100 most highly cited articles in disciplinary journals 2000–2009.' *British Journal of Social Work 6,* 19, 765–782.

Holman, C. D., Bass, A. J., Rosman, D. L., Smith, M. B. *et al.* (2008) 'A decade of data linkage in Western Australia: Strategic design, applications and benefits of the WA data linkage system.' *Australian Health Review 32,* 4, 766–777.

Holzer, P. J., Higgins, J. R., Bromfield, L. M., Richardson, N. and Higgins, D. J. (2006) 'The effectiveness of parent education and home visiting child maltreatment prevention programs.' *Child Abuse Prevention Issues 24.*

Honkatukia, P., Nyqvist, L. and Pösö, T. (2006) 'Violence from within the reform schools.' *Youth Violence and Juvenile Justice 4,* 4, 328–344.

Hooper, C. A., Gorin, S., Cabral, C. and Dyson, C. (2007) *Living with Hardship 24/7: The Diverse Experiences of Families in Poverty in England.* London: The Frank Buttle Trust.

Horrell, S. and Humphries, J. (1995) 'The exploitation of little children: Child labor and the family economy in the industrial revolution.' *Explorations in Economic History 32,* 4, 485–516.

Horwath, J. (2007) *Child Neglect: Identification and Assessment.* Basingstoke: Palgrave Macmillan.

Horwath, J. and Morrison, T. (2001) 'Assessment of Parental Motivation to Change.' In J. Horwath (ed.) *The Child's World.* London: Jessica Kingsley Publishers.

Howard, K. S. and Brooks-Gunn, J. (2009) 'The role of home-visiting programs in preventing child abuse and neglect'. *The Future of Children 19,* 2, 119–146.

Howe, D. (1994) 'Modernity, postmodernity and social work.' *British Journal of Social Work 24,* 5, 13–532.

Howe, D. (2010) 'The safety of children and the parent–worker relationship in cases of child abuse and neglect.' Child Abuse Review 19, 5, 330–341.

Howe, D., Brandon, M., Hinings, D. and Schofield, G. (1999) *Attachment Theory, Child Maltreatment and Family Support: A Practice and Assessment Model.* London: Macmillan.

Human Rights Watch (2006) *Sri Lanka: Stop Child Abductions by Karuna Group.* New York, NY: Human Rights Watch. Available at www.hrw.org/news/2006/11/27/sri-lanka-stop-child-abductions-karuna-group, accessed 24 March 2015.

Humphreys, C. and Absler, D. (2011) 'History repeating: Child protection responses to domestic violence.' *Child and Family Social Work 16,* 464–473.

Humppi, S. and Ellonen, N., (2010) *Lapsiin Kohdistuva Väkivalta ja Hyväksikäyttö – Tapausten Tunnistaminen, Rikosprosessi ja Viranomaisten Yhteistyö [Violence and Exploitation Targeted to Children: Identifying the Cases, Legal Process and Authorities' Cooperation].* Tampere: Police College of Finland.

Hurtig, J. (2013) *Taivaan Taimet: Uskonnollinen Yhteisöllisyys ja Väkivalta [The Seedlings of Heaven: Religious Community and Violence].* Tampere: Vastapaino.

Husso, M., Vikki, T., Notko, M., Holma, J., Laitila, A. and Mäntysaari, M. (2012) 'Making sense of domestic violence intervention in professional health care.' *Health and Social Care in the Community 20*, 4, 347–355.

Institute of Medicine and National Research Council (2014) *New Directions in Child Abuse and Neglect Research.* Washington, DC: The National Academies Press.

Jäntti, M. (2010) 'Lapsiköyhyydestä Suomessa [About Child Poverty in Finland].' In U. Hämäläinen and O. Kangas (eds) *Perhepiirissä [Within the Family Circle].* Helsinki: Kelan Tutkimusosasto.

Jeffreys, H., Hirte, C., Rogers, N. and Wilson, R. (2009) *Parental Substance Misuse and Children's Entry into Alternative Care in South Australia.* Adelaide: Department for Families and Communities.

Kaime, T. (2011) *The Convention on the Rights of the Child: A Cultural Legitimacy Critique.* Groningen: Europa Law Publishing.

Kataja, K., Ristikari, T., Paananen, R., Heino, T. and Gissler, M. (2014) 'Hyvinvointiongelmien ylisukupolviset jatkumot kodin ulkopuolelle sijoitettujen lasten elämässä' [Intergenerational inheritance of welfare problems among children placed outside their homes]. *Yhteiskuntapolitiikka 79*, 1, 38–53.

Kavapalu, H. (1993) 'Dealing with the dark side in the ethnography of childhood: child punishment in Tonga.' *Oceania 63*, 4, 313–329.

Kelman, C. W., Bass, A. J. and Holman, C. D. (2002) 'Research use of linked health data: a best practice protocol.' *Australian and New Zealand Journal of Public Health 26*, 3, 251–255.

Kempe, C. H., Silverman, F., Steele, B., Droegemueller, W. and Silver, H. (1962), 'The battered child syndrome.' *Journal of the American Medical Association 181*, 4–11.

Keskinen, S. (2005) *Perheammattilaiset ja Väkivaltatyön Ristiriidat: Sukupuoli, Valta ja Kielelliset Käytännöt [Family Professionals and Discrepancies of Working with Violence: Gender, Power and Discursive Practices].* Tampere: Tampere University Press.

Ki-moon, B. (2013) *A Life of Dignity for All: Accelerating Progress Towards the Millennium Development Goals and Advancing the United Nations Development Agenda Beyond 2015 (Report of the Secretary-General A/68/202).* New York: United Nations. Available at www.un.org/millenniumgoals/pdf/A%20Life%20of%20Dignity%20for%20All.pdf, accessed 17 March 2015.

Koponen, A., Kalland, M., Autti-Rämä, I., Laamanen, R. and Suominen, S. (2013) 'Socio-emotional development of children with foetal alcohol spectrum disorders in long-term foster family care: a qualitative study.' *Nordic Social Work Research 3*,1, 38–58.

Krug, E. G., Dahlberg, L. L., Mercy, J. A., Zwi, A. B. and Lozano, R. (2002) *World Report on Violence and Health.* Geneva: World Health Organization.

Krugman, R. D. and Korbin, J. E. (eds) (2013) *C. Henry Kempe: A 50 Year Legacy to the Field of Child Abuse and Neglect.* Dordrecht: Springer.

Kyte, A., Trocmé, N. and Chamberland, C. (2013) 'Evaluating where we're at with differential response.' *Child Abuse and Neglect 37*, 125–132.

Laitinen, M. (2004) *Häväistyt Ruumiit, Rikotut Mielet [Disgraced Bodies, Broken Minds].* Tampere: Vastapaino.

Laming, W. H. (2003) *The Victoria Climbié Inquiry: Report of an Inquiry by Lord Laming (Cm5730).* London: The Stationery Office.

Landgren, K. (2005) 'The protective environment: Development support for child protection.' *Human Rights Quarterly 27*, 1, 214–248.

Lapierre, S. (2010) 'More responsibilities, less control: Understanding the challenges and difficulties involved in mothering in the context of domestic violence.' *British Journal of Social Work 40*, 1434–1451.

Laplanche, J. (1999) *Essays on Otherness.* London: Routledge.

Lea, A. (2011) *Families with Complex Needs: A Review of the Current Literature.* Leicester: Leicestershire County Council.

Lee, N. (2001), *Childhood and Society: Growing up in an Age of Uncertainty*. Buckingham: Open University Press.

Lees, A. (2014) 'Spotlights and Shadows: A Social Work Perspective on Information Sharing to Safeguard Children' [unpublished PhD thesis]. Southampton: University of Southampton.

Lewig, K., Arney, F. and Salveron, M. (2010) 'Challenges to parenting in a new culture: Implications for child and family welfare.' *Evaluation and Program Planning 33*, 3, 324–332.

Lewig, K., Arney, F., Salveron, M., McLaren, H., Gibson, C. and Scott, D. (2010) 'Spreading Promising Ideas and Innovations in Child and Family Services.' In F. Arney and D. Scott (eds) *Working with Vulnerable Families: A Partnership Approach*. Melbourne: Cambridge University Press.

Lewis, G., Kirkham, H., Duncan, I. and Vaithianathan, R. (2013) 'How health systems could avert "triple fail" events that are harmful, are costly, and result in poor patient satisfaction.' *Health Affairs 32*, 4, 669–676.

Lexmond, J., Bazalgette, L. and Margo, J. (2011) *The Home Front*. London: Demos.

Local Government Association (2013) *Future Funding Outlook for Councils from 2010/11 to 2019/20*. London: Local Government Association.

Locke, J. (1982) *Second Treatise of Government*. Arlington Heights, IL: Harlan Davidson Inc. (Original work published 1690.)

Long, T., Murphy, M., Fallon, D., Livesley, J. *et al.* (2012) *Evaluation of the Action for Children UK Neglect Project*. Manchester: Salford University.

Machel, G. (1996) *Impact of Armed Conflict on Children (Report of Graça Machel, Expert of the Secretary-General of the United Nations)*. New York: United Nations, Unicef. Available at www.unicef.org/graca, accessed 17 March 2015.

Macmillan, H. L., Jamieson, E., Wathen, C. N., Boyle, M. H. *et al.* (2007) 'Development of a policy-relevant child maltreatment research strategy.' *Milbank Quarterly 85*, 2, 337–374.

Magone, C., Neuman, M. and Weissman, F. (eds) (2011) *Humanitarian Negotiations Revealed: The MSF Experience* London: Hurst and Company.

Magus, P., Irgens, L. M., Huag, K., Nystad, W. *et al.* (2006) 'Cohort profile: The Norwegian Motehr and Child Cohort Study (MoBa).' *International Journal of Epidemiology 35*, 5, 1146–1150.

Malinowski, B. (1922) *Argonauts of the Western Pacific: An Account of Native Enterprise and Adventure in the Archipelagoes of Melanesian New Guinea*. London: Routledge.

Malinowski, B. (1967) *A Diary in the Strict Sense of the Term*. London: Routledge and Kegan Paul.

Marcenko, M. O., Lyons, S. and Courtney, M. (2011) 'Mothers' experiences, resources and needs: The context for reunification.' *Children and Youth Services Review 33*, 431–438.

Marsh, P. and Fisher, M. in collaboration with Mathers, N. and Fish, S. (2005) *Developing the Evidence Base for Social Work and Social Care Practice: Using Knowledge in Social Care Report 10*. London: Social Care Institute for Excellence. Available at www.scie.org.uk/publications/reports/report10.pdf, accessed 24 March 2015.

Marshall, T. H. (1950), *Citizenship and Social Class and Other Essays*. Cambridge: University of Cambridge Press.

Maslow, A. H. (1943) 'A theory of human motivation.' *Psychological Review 50*, 4, 370–396.

Mattinson, J. and Sinclair, I. (1979) *Mate and Stalemate*. London: Tavistock Institute of Medical Psychology.

Maynard, T. and Thomas, N. (2009) *An Introduction to Early Childhood Studies*. London: Sage.

McDonald, M., Higgins, D., Valentine, K. and Lamont, A. (2011) *Protecting Australia's Children Research Audit*. Melbourne: Australian Institute of Family Studies.

McDougall, S. and Gibson, C. (2014) 'Advancing visibility of the child in adult and child and family services.' *Communities, Children and Families Australia 8*, 1, 21–35.

McGavock, L. (2012) 'Adverse Childhood Experiences of an Undergraduate Population in Northern Ireland: Associations with Educational Pathways and Social Service Contact' [unpublished PhD thesis]. Belfast: The McClay library, Queen's University Belfast.

McGavock, L. and Spratt, T. (2014) 'Prevalence of adverse childhood experiences in a university population: Associations with use of social services.' *British Journal of Social Work 44*, 3, 675–693.

McGillivray, A. (1994) 'Why children do have equal rights: in reply to Laura Purdy.' *International Journal of Children's Rights 2*, 3, 243–258.

McGuinness, K. and Arney, F. (2012) *Foster and Kinship Care Recruitment Campaigns: A Review and synthesis of the Literature.* Darwin: Menzies School of Health Research.

McIntyre, A. (ed.) (2005) 'Introduction to Her.' In *Invisible Stakeholders: Children and War in Africa.* Pretoria: Institute of Security Studies.

Mearsheimer, J. and Walt, S. (2007) *The Israel Lobby and US Foreign Policy.* New York, NY: Farrar, Straus and Giroux.

Menzies Lyth, I. (1988) 'A Case Study in the Functioning of Social Systems as a Defence Against Anxiety.' In *Containing Anxiety in Institutions: Selected Essays Volume 1.* London: Free Association Books.

Mikton, C. and Butchart, A (2009) 'Child maltreatment prevention: a systematic review of reviews.' *Bulletin of World Health Organization 87*, 354, 353–361.

Mildon, R. and Shlonsky, A. (2011) 'Bridge over troubled water: Using implementation science to facilitate effective services in child welfare.' *Child Abuse and Neglect 35*, 9, 753–756.

Mildon, R., Bromfield, L., Arney, F., Lewig, K., Michaux, A. and Antcliff, G. (2012) 'Facilitating Evidence-Informed Practice: Participatory Knowledge Translation and Exchange.' In K. Dill and W. Shera (eds) *Facilitating Evidence-Informed Practice: International Perspectives.* Toronto, Canada: Canadian Scholars' Press.

Ministry of Justice (2013) *8-vuotiaan Lapsen Kuolemaan Johtaneet Tapahtumat [Events Leading to the Death of an Eight-year old Child in Helsinki in May 2012].* Report and Guidelines 32. Helsinki: Ministry of Justice.

Ministry of Social Affairs and Health (2013) *Toimiva Lastensuojelu. [Functioning Child Welfare].* Report 19. Helsinki: Ministry of Social Affairs and Health.

Ministry of the Interior (2008) *Safety first: Internal Security Programme: Government Plenary Session 8 May 2008. Publications 25.* Helsinki: Ministry of the Interior.

Ministry of the Interior (2012) *Selvitys Perhe- ja Lapsensurmien Taustoista Vuosilta 2003–2012 [Review of the Backgrounds for Familicide and Filicide in 2003–2012]. Publications of Ministry of Interior 35.* Helsinki: Ministry of Interior.

Montgomery, H. (2013) 'Childhood: An Anthropological Approach.' In M.-J. Kehily (ed.) *Understanding Childhood: A Cross-Disciplinary Approach.* Bristol: Policy Press.

Moore, T. and McArthur, M. (2011) '"Good for Kids": Children who have been homeless talk about school.' *Australian Journal of Education 55*, 2, 147–160.

Morton, H. (1996) *Becoming Tongan: An Ethnography of Childhood.* Honolulu: University of Hawaii Press.

Mudaly, N. and Goddard, C. (2006) *The Truth is Longer than a Lie: Children's Experiences of Abuse and Professional Interventions.* London: Jessica Kingsley Publishers.

Mulley, C. (2009) *The Woman Who Saved the Children.* Oxford: One World.

Munro, E. (2007) 'The dangers of information sharing.' *Social Policy Journal of New Zealand 31*, 41–55.

Munro, E. (2010) *The Munro Review of Child Protection. Part One: A Systems Analysis.* London: Department for Education. Available at www.gov.uk/government/publications/munro-review-of-child-protection-part-1-a-systems-analysis, accessed 24 March 2015.

Munro, E. (2011a) *The Munro Review of Child Protection Interim Report: The Child's Journey.* London: Department for Education. Available at www.gov.uk/government/publications/munro-review-of-child-protection-interim-report-the-childs-journey, accessed 24 March 2015.

Munro, E. (2011b) *The Munro Review of Child Protection: Final Report: A Child-Centred System.* London: The Stationery Office. Available at www.gov.uk/government/publications/munro-review-of-child-protection-final-report-a-child-centred-system, accessed 24 March 2015.

Narey, M. 2014. *Making the Education of Social Workers Consistently Effective: Report of Sir Martin Narey's Independent Review of the Education of Children's Social Workers.* London: Department for Education.

Nations, M. K. and Rebhun, L. A. (1988) 'Angels with wet wings won't fly: Maternal sentiment in Brazil and the image of neglect.' *Culture, Medicine and Psychiatry, 12,* 2, 141–200.

New Zealand Government (n.d.) *The White Paper for Vulnerable Children.* Volume II. Available at www.msd.govt.nz/documents/about-msd-and-our-work/work-programmes/policy-development/white-paper-vulnerable-children/whitepaper-volume-ii-web.pdf, accessed 12 May 2015.

Nietzsche, F. (1969) *On the Genealogy of Morals* (trans. W. Kaufmann). New York, NY: Random House.

Northern Territory Government (2010) *Growing Them Strong, Together: Promoting the safety and wellbeing of the Northern Territory's children: Report of the Board of Inquiry into the Child Protection System in the Northern Territory 2010.* Darwin, NT: Northern Territory Government.

Notermans, C. (2008) 'The emotional world of kinship: Children's experiences of fosterage in East Cameroon.' *Childhood 15,* 3, 355–277.

Noyes C. (unpublished) 'Live Work: Creativity at the Front Line' [doctoral research in progress]. London: Tavistock Centre/University of East London.

NSPCC (2008) *Poverty and Child Maltreatment: Child Protection Research Briefing.* London: NSPCC.

Nussbaum, M. (2011) *Creating Capabilities: The Human Development Approach.* Harvard, MA: Harvard University Press.

O'Donnell, M., Anderson, D., Morgan, V. A., Nassar, N., Leonard, H. and Stanley, J. (2013) 'Increasing trends of pre-existing mental health disorders in parents of infants born between 1990 and 2005.' *Medical Journal of Australia 198,* 485–488.

O'Donnell, M., Nassar, N., Jacoby, P. and Stanley, F. (2012) 'Western Australian emergency department admissions related to child maltreatment and intentional injury: Population level study utilising linked health and child protection data.' *Journal of Paediatrics and Child Health 48,* 57–65.

O'Donnell, M., Nassar, N., Leonard, H., Hagan, R. *et al.* (2009) 'Increasing prevalence of neonatal withdrawal syndrome: Population study of maternal factors and child protection involvement.' *Pediatrics 123,* 4, e614–e621.

O'Donnell, M., Nassar, N., Leonard, H., Mathews, R., Patterson, Y. and Stanley, F. (2010a) 'Monitoring child abuse and neglect at a population level: Patterns of hospital admissions for maltreatment and assault.' *Child Abuse and Neglect 34,* 823–832.

O'Donnell, M., Nassar, N., Leonard, H., Mathews, R., Patterson, Y. and Stanley, F. (2010b) 'The use of cross-jurisdictional population data to investigate health indicators of child maltreatment.' *Medical Journal of Australia 193,* 142–145.

O'Donnell, M., Scott, D. and Stanley, F. (2008) 'Child abuse and neglect: Is it time for a public health approach?' *Australian and New Zealand Journal of Public Health 32,* 4, 325–330.

OECD (2011) *Family Database.* Available at www.oecd.org/els/soc/database.htm, accessed 30 April 2015. Cited in Gilbert, R., Fluke, J., O'Donnell, M., Gonzalez-Izquierdo, A. *et al.* (2012) 'Child maltreatment: variation in trends and policies in six developed countries.' *Lancet 379,* 758–772.

Oelkers, J. (2005), *Reformpädagogik: Eine kritische Dogmengeschichte.* Weinheim: Juventa.

Olds, D. L. (2006) 'The nurse–family partnership: An evidence-based preventive intervention.' *Infant Mental Health Journal 27*, 1, 5–25.

Olds, D. L., Eckenrode, J., Henderson, C. R. J. *et al.* (1997) 'Long-term Effects of Home Visitation on Maternal Life Course and Child Abuse and Neglect: Fifteen-Year Followup of a Randomised Trial.' *JAMA, 278*, 8, 637–643.

Osborn, A. and Bromfield, L. (2007) 'Outcomes for children and young people in care.' *National Child Protection Clearinghouse Research Brief.* Melbourne: Australian Institute of Family Studies.

Øverlien, C. (2010) 'Children exposed to domestic violence: conclusions from the literature and challenges ahead.' *Journal of Social Work 10*, 1, 80–97.

Paavilainen, E. and Flinck, A. (2014) 'The effectiveness of methods designed to identify child maltreatment in social and health care: A systematic review protocol.' *PROSPERO 2014*, CRD42014008770. Available at www.crd.york.ac.uk/PROSPERO/display_record. asp?ID=CRD42014008770, accessed 25 March 2015.

Paavilainen, E., Lepistö, S. and Flinck, A. (2014) 'Ethical issues in family violence research in health care settings.' *Nursing Ethics 21*,1, 43–52.

Parker, R. and Aggleton, P. (2002) 'Hiv/Aids-related stigma and discrimination: A conceptual framework and an agenda for action.' *Social Science and Medicine 57*, 1, 1–28.

Parry, Y., Maio-Taddeo, C., Arnold, L. and Nayda, R. (2009) *Professionals Protecting Children: Child Protection and Nursing and Midwifery Education in Australia.* Adelaide: Australian Centre for Child Protection.

Parton, N. (2011) 'Child protection and safeguarding in England: Changing and competing conceptions of risk and their implications for social work'. *British Journal of Social Work 41*, 854–875.

Parton, N. (2014) *The Politics of Child Protection.* Basingstoke: Palgrave Macmillan.

Peltonen, K. (2011) *Children and Violence: Nature, Consequences and Interventions.* Tampere: Tampere University Press.

Perlman, H. H. (1957) *Social Casework: A Problem-Solving Process.* Chicago, IL: University of Chicago Press.

Petrie, P. (2013) 'Social pedagogy in the UK: Gaining a firm foothold?' *Education Policy Analysis Archives 21*, 37, 1–16.

Pinheiro, P. S. (2006) *United Nations World Report on Violence Against Children: United Nations Secretary-General's Study on Violence against Children.* New York: United Nations. Available at www.unicef. org/violencestudy/reports.html, accessed 17 March 2015.

Pösö, T. (1997) 'Finland: Child Abuse as a Family Problem.' In N. Gilbert (ed.) *Combatting Child Abuse: International Perspectives and Trends.* Oxford: Oxford University Press.

Pösö, T. (2011) 'Combatting Child Abuse in Finland: From Family to Child-Centered Orientation.' In N. Gilbert, N. Parton and M. Skivenes (eds) *Child Protection Systems. International Trends and Orientations.* New York, NY: Oxford University Press.

Power, M. (2004) *The Risk Management of Everything: Rethinking the Politics of Uncertainty.* London: Demos.

Price-Robertson, R., Bromfield, L. and Vassallo, S. (2010) 'Prevalence matters: Estimating the extent of child maltreatment in Australia.' *Developing Practice 26*, 12–20.

Prinz, R. J., Sanders, M. R., Shapiro, C. J., Whitaker, D. J. and Lutzker, J. R. (2009) 'Population-based prevention of child maltreatment: The U.S. Triple P system population trial.' *Prevention Science 10*, 1–12.

Pritchard, C. and Williams, R. (2010) 'Comparing possible "child-abuse-related-deaths" in England and Wales with the major developed countries 1974–2006: Signs of Progress?' *British Journal of Social Work 40*, 6, 1700–1718.

Productivity Commission (2014) 'Report on Government Services.' Canberra: Commonwealth of Australia.

Putnam-Hornstein, E., Webster, D., Needell, B. and Magruder, J. (2011) 'A public health approach to child maltreatment surveillance: Evidence from a data linkage project in the United States.' *Child Abuse Review 20*, 256–273.

Radford, L., Corral, S., Bradley, C., Fisher, H. *et al.* (2011) *Child Abuse and Neglect in the UK Today.* London: NSPCC.

Read, K. (2001) 'When is a kid a kid? Negotiating children's rights in El Salvador's civil war.' *History of Religions 41*, 4, 391–409.

Reading, R., Bissell, S., Goldhagen, J. Harwin, J. *et al.* (2009) 'Promotion of children's rights and prevention of child maltreatment.' *Lancet 373*, 332–343.

Research Assessment Exercises (RAE) (2008) Available at www.rae.ac.uk/results/qualityProfile. aspx?id=40&type=uoa, accessed on 9 June 2015.

Research Assessment Exercises (RAE) (2001) Available at http://www.rae.ac.uk/2001/results/ byuoa/51.htm, accessed on 9 June 2015.

Renne, E. (2005) 'Childhood memories and contemporary parenting in Ekiti, Nigeria.' *Africa, 75*, 1, 63–82.

Rhodes, A. E., Boyle, M. H., Bethell, J., Wekerle, C. *et al.* (2012) 'Child maltreatment and onset of emergency department presentations for suicide-related behaviours.' *Child Abuse and Neglect 36*, 542–551.

Roos, L. L., Brownell, M., Lix, L., Roos, N. P., Walld, R. and MacWilliam, L. (2008) 'From health research to social research: Privacy, methods, approaches.' *Social Science and Medicine 66*, 1, 117–129.

Royal Commission into Institutional Responses to Child Sexual Abuse (2014) *Interim Report: Volume 1.* Canberra, Commonwealth of Australia.

Ruch, G., Turney, D. and Ward, A. (2010) *Relationship-based Social Work: Getting to the Heart of Practice.* London: Jessica Kingsley Publishers.

Rustin, M. (2005) 'Conceptual analysis of critical moments in Victoria Climbié's life.' Child and Family Social Work 10, 11–19.

Ryan, G. (2013) 'Henry.' In R. D. Krugman and J. E. Korbin (eds) *C. Henry Kempe: A 50 Year Legacy to the Field of Child Abuse and Neglect.* Dordrecht: Springer.

Salmivalli, C. and Poskiparta, E. (2012) 'KiVa antibullying program: Overview of evaluation studies based on a randomized controlled trial and national rollout in Finland.' *International Journal of Conflict and Violence 6*, 2, 294–302.

Salveron, M. and Arney, F. (2013) 'Understanding the journey of parents whose children are in out-of-home care.' In F. Arney and D. Scott (eds) *Working with Vulnerable Families: A Partnership Approach* (2nd edition). Melbourne: Cambridge University Press.

Salveron, M., Lewig, K. and Arney, F. (2009) 'Parenting groups for parents whose children are in care.' *Child Abuse Review 18*, 4, 267–288.

Sandel, M. (1982) *Liberalism and the Limits of Justice.* Cambridge: Cambridge University Press.

Sariola, H. (1990) *Lasten Väkivalta- ja Seksuaalikokemukset [Children's Experiences of Violence at Home].* Helsinki: Lastensuojelun Keskusliitto.

Saunders, V. and McArthur, M. (2013) *Children of Prisoners: Exploring the Needs of Children and Young People Who Have a Parent Incarcerated in the ACT.* Canberra: SHINE for Kids.

Save the Children (2007) *Child Protection in Emergencies: Priorities, Principles and Practices* Stockholm: International Save the Children Alliance.

Save the Children Sweden (2006) *Child Rights Programming* (2nd edition). Stockholm: Save the Children Sweden. Available at http://resourcecentre.savethechildren.se/sites/default/files/ documents/2658.pdf, accessed 25 March 2015.

Scheper-Hughes, N. (1992) *Death Without Weeping: The Violence of Everyday Life in Brazil.* Berkeley, CA: University of California Press.

Scheper-Hughes, N. and Bourgois, P. (eds) (2004) *Violence in War and Peace: An Anthology*. Oxford: Basil Blackwell.

Schmid, J. (2015) 'Overlooking the most vulnerable: The child welfare research agenda 2005–2010.' *European Journal of Social Work 18*, 1, 6–16.

Schulman, S., Curtis, C. and Vanstone, C. (2011) 'Family by Family: A Co-designed and Co-produced Family Support Model.' In K. Brettig and M. Sims (eds) *Building Integrated Connections for Children, their Families and Communities*. Newcastle upon Tyne: Cambridge Scholars Publishing.

Scott, D. (2006) 'Towards a public health model of child protection in Australia.' *Communities, Children and Families Australia 1*, 1, 9–16.

Scott, D. (2009) 'Think child, think family: How adult specialist services can support children at risk of abuse and neglect.' *Family Matters 81*, 37–42.

Scottish Government (2010) *National Guidance on Child Protection in Scotland*. Edinburgh: Scottish Government. Available at www.scotland.gov.uk/Publications/2010/12/09134441/0, accessed 25 March 2015.

Scourfield, J. B. (2001) 'Constructing women in child protection work.' *Child and Family Social Work 6*, 77–87.

Segal, L., Dalziel, K. and Papandrea, K. (2013) 'Report as Appendix F: Where to Invest to Reduce Child Maltreatment: A Decision Framework and Evidence from the International Literature.' In Queensland Child Protection Commission of Inquiry *Taking Responsibility: A Roadmap for Queensland Child Protection*. Cairns: Queensland Child Protection Commission of Inquiry.

Sen, A. (2009) *The Idea of Justice*. Cambridge, MA: Harvard University Press.

Sen, A. K. (2005) 'Human rights and capabilities.' *Journal of Human Development 6*, 2, 151–166.

Sethi, D., Bellis, M., Hughes, K., Gilbert, R., Mitis, F. and Galea, G. (2013) *European Report on Preventing Child Maltreatment*. Denmark: World Health Organization Regional Office for Europe.

Sharland, E. (2009) *Strategic Advisor for Social Work and Social Care Research: Main Report to the Economic and Social Research Council Training and Development Board*. Brighton: University of Sussex. Available at www.esrc.ac.uk/_images/Main_report_SW_and_SC_tcm8-4647.pdf, accessed 25 March 2015.

Shaw, I. and Norton, M. (2008) 'Kinds and quality of social work research.' *British Journal of Social Work 38*, 953–970.

Shaw, T. (2007) *Historic Abuse Systemic Review: Residential Schools and Children's Homes in Scotland 1950–1995*. Edinburgh: Scottish Government.

Sheldon, B. and Macdonald, G. (2009) *A Textbook of Social Work*. London: Routledge.

Shlonsky, A. and Wagner, D. (2005) 'The next step: Integrating actuarial assessment and clinical judgement into an evidence-based practice framework in CPS case management.' *Children and Youth Services Review 27*, 409–427.

Shonkoff, J. P. and Garner, A. S. (2012) 'The lifelong effects of early childhood adversity and toxic stress. *Pediatrics 129*, 232–246.

Sidebotham, P., Atkins, B. and Hutton, J. L. (2012) 'Changes in rates of violent child deaths in England and Wales between 1974–2008: An analysis of national mortality data.' *Archives of Disease in Childhood 97*, 193–99.

Snow, J., Frost, W. H. and Richardson, B. W. (1936) *Snow on Cholera*. New York, NY: Commonwealth Fund.

Spencer, N. and Baldwin, N. (2005) 'Economic, Cultural and Social Contexts of Neglect.' In J. Taylor and B. Daniel (eds) *Child Neglect: Practice Issues for Health and Social Care*. London: Jessica Kingsley Publishers.

Spratt, T. (2001) 'The influence of child protection practice orientation on child welfare practice.' *British Journal of Social Work 31*, 933–954.

Spratt, T. (2012) 'Why multiples matter: Reconceptualising the population referred to child and family social workers.' *British Journal of Social Work 42*, 8, 1574–1591.

Stanley, N., Miller, P., Richardson Foster, H. and Tomson, G. (2010) *Children and Families Experiencing Domestic Violence: Police and Children's Social Services' Responses.* London: NSPCC and University of Central Lancashire.

Stateva, M., Minton, J., Beckett, C., Doolan, M. *et al.* (2006) 'Challenges recruiting families with children at risk of anti-social behaviour into intervention trials: lessons from the Helping Children Achieve study.' *Journal of Children's Services 7*, 4, 285–302.

Stevens, I. and Cox, P. (2008) 'Complexity theory: Developing new understandings of child protection and in residential care.' *British Journal of Social Work 338*, 7, 1320–1336.

Stevenson, O. (1986) 'Guest editorial on the Jasmine Beckford Inquiry.' *British Journal of Social Work 16*, 501–510.

Stevenson, O. (1998) *Neglected Children: Issues and Dilemmas.* Oxford: Blackwell.

Stoecklin, D. and Bonvin, J.-M. (2014) *Children's Rights and the Capability Approach: Challenges and Prospects.* Dordrecht: Springer.

Sykes, J. (2011) 'Negotiating stigma: Understanding mothers' responses to accusations of child neglect.' *Children and Youth Services Review 33*, 3, 448–456.

Taylor, B. (2010) *Professional Decision Making in Social Work Practice.* Exeter: Learning Matters.

Terre des Hommes (2011) *Enhancing Child Protection Systems.* Lausanne: Tdh. Available at http://resourcecentre.savethechildren.se/sites/default/files/documents/5473.pdf, accessed 25 March 2015.

The Protection Project and ICMEC (2013) *Child Protection Model Law.* Washington: The Protection Project and International Centre for Missing and Exploited Children. Available at www.protectionproject.org/wp-content/uploads/2014/01/Best-Practices-in-Child-Protection-2013.pdf, accessed 25 March 2015.

Tilbury, C. (2009) 'A "stock and flow" analysis of Australian child protection data.' *Communities, Children and Families Australia 4*, 2, 9–17.

Tisdall, E. K. M. and Davis, J. M. (2015) 'Children's Rights and Wellbeing: Tensions within the Children and Young People (Scotland) Act 2014.' In A. Smith (ed.) *Enhancing the Rights and Wellbeing of Children: Connecting Research, Policy and Practice.* Basingstoke: Palgrave Macmillan.

Toasland, J. (2007) 'Containing the container: An exploration of the containing role of management in a social work context.' *Journal of Social Work Practice 21*, 2, 197–202.

Tomison, A. M. and Poole, L. (2000) *Preventing Child Abuse and Neglect: Findings from an Australian Audit of Prevention Programs.* Melbourne: Australian Institute of Family Studies.

Towle, C. (1946) 'Social Casework in Modern Society.' *Social Service Review 20*, 1/4,165–179.

Trutwein, B. and Rosman, D. L. (2006) 'Health data linkage conserves privacy in a research-rich environment.' *Annals of Epidemiology 16*, 4, 279–280.

UNICEF (2004) *A Principled Approach to Humanitarian Action: PATH Training Programme.* Available at www.unicef.org/pathtraining/programmeguide.htm, accessed 25 March 2015.

UNICEF (2006) Child Protection Information Sheet. What is Child Protection? New York: UNICEF. Available at www.unicef.org/chinese/protection/files/Child_Protection_Information_Sheets_(Booklet).pdf, accessed 25 March 2015.

UNICEF (2013) *A Better Way to Protect All Children: The Theory and Practice of Child Protection Systems* New York: UNICEF. Available at www.streetchildrenresources.org/wp-content/uploads/2013/09/A-better-way-to-protect-all-children.pdf, accessed 25 March 2015.

United Nations (1989) *Convention on the Rights of the Child.* Geneva: United Nations. Available at www.ohchr.org/en/professionalinterest/pages/crc.aspx, accessed 25 March 2015.

United Nations Children's Fund (2014) *Hidden in Plain Sight: A Statistical Analysis of Violence Against Children.* New York: UNICEF.

United Nations Committee on the Rights of the Child (UNCRC) (2003) *General Comment No. 5: General Measures of Implementation of the Convention on the Rights of the Child.* Geneva: United Nations. Available at http://tbinternet.ohchr.org/_layouts/treatybodyexternal/Download.aspx?symbolno=CRC%2fGC%2f2003%2f5&Lang=en, accessed 25 March 2015.

UNCRC (2011) *General Comment No. 13: The Right of the Child to Freedom From All Forms Of Violence.* Geneva: United Nations. Available at www2.ohchr.org/english/bodies/crc/docs/CRC.C.GC.13_en.pdf, accessed 25 March 2015.

United Nations Secretary-General (2006) *World Report on Violence against Children.* Geneva: United Nations. Available at www.unviolencestudy.org/, accessed 25 March 2015.

Urwin, C. and Sternberg, J. (eds) (2012) *Infant Observation and Research: Emotional processes in Everyday Life.* Hove: Routledge.

Vaithianathan, R., Dare, T., Maloney, T., Jiang, N. *et al.* (2012) *Ministry of Social Development Research Report: Vulnerable Children: Can Administrative Data be Used to Identify Children at Risk of Adverse Outcomes.* Auckland: Centre for Applied Research in Economics (CARE), Department of Economics, University of Auckland. Available at www.msd.govt.nz/documents/about-msd-and-our-work/publications-resources/research/vulnerable-children/auckland-university-can-administrative-data-be-used-to-identify-children-at-risk-of-adverse-outcome.pdf, accessed 25 March 2015.

Vaithianathan, R., Maloney, T., Putnam-Hornstein, E. and Jiang, N. (2013) 'Children in the public benefit system at risk of maltreatment: Identification via predictive modeling.' *American Journal of Preventive Medicine 45*, 3, 354–359.

Valentin, K. and Meinert, L. (2009) 'The adult north and the young south.' *Anthropology Today 25*, 3, 23–28.

Wade, J., Biehal, N., Farrelly, N. and Sinclair, I. (2010) *Maltreated Children in the Looked After System: A Comparison of Outcomes for Those Who Go Home and Those Who Do Not.* London: Department for Children, Schools and Families.

Wagner, P. (1994) *A Sociology of Modernity: Liberty and Discipline.* London: Routledge.

Waldfogel, J. (2009) 'Prevention and the child protection system.' *The Future of Children 19*, 2, 195–210.

Ward, H., Brown, R., Westlake, D. and Munro, E. R. (2010) *Report to Department of Education: Infants Suffering, or Likely to Suffer, Significant Harm: A Prospective Longitudinal Study.* Loughborough: CCFR, Loughborough University.

Waterhouse, L. and McGhee, J. (2014) 'Agamben and the political positioning of child welfare-involved mothers in child protective services.' *Families, Relationships and Societies.* Available at www.ingentaconnect.com/content/tpp/frs/pre-prints/content-PP_FRS-D-14-00006R2, accessed 30 April 2015.

Waters, H. (1995) 'The great famine and the rise of anti-Irish racism.' *Race and Class 37*, 1, 95–107.

Weber, M. (1947) *The Theory of Social and Economic Organization.* New York, NY: Hodge.

Wells, K. (2009) *Childhood in a Global Perspective.* Bristol: Policy Press.

Whittaker, A. (2011) 'Social defences and organisational culture in a local authority child protection setting: challenges for the Munro Review?' *Journal of Social Work Practice 25*, 4, 481–495.

Wilkinson, R. and Pickett, K. (2009) *The Spirit Level: Why More Equal Societies Always Do Better.* London: Penguin.

Wilson, J. M. G., Jungne, G. (1968) *Principles and Practice of Screening for Disease.* Geneva: World Health Organization.

Wilson, J. M. G. and Jungner, G. (1968) *Principles and Practice of Screening for Disease.* Geneva: World Health Organization. Available at http://whqlibdoc.who.int/php/WHO_PHP_34.pdf, accessed 25 March 2015.

Wolock, I. and Horowitz, B. (1984) 'Child maltreatment as a social problem: The neglect of neglect.' *The American Journal of Orthopsychiatry 54*, 4, 530–543.

World Health Organization (2002) *World Report on Violence and Health: Summary.* Geneva, World
      Health Organization. Available at www.who.int/violence_injury_prevention/violence/
      world_report/en/, accessed 17 March 2015.

World Health Organization Regional Office for Europe. (2010) *Better Health, Better Lives: Children
      and Young Children with Intellectual Disabilities and Their Families.* Copenhagen: World Health
      Organization Regional Office for Europe.

Wulczyn, F. (2009) 'Epidemiological perspectives on maltreatment prevention.' *Future Child 19*
      39–66, cited in Gilbert, R., Fluke, J., O'Donnell, M., Gonzalez-Izquierdo, A. *et al.* (2012)
      'Child maltreatment: variation in trends and policies in six developed countries.' *Lancet 379*,
      758–772.

Zertal, I. and Eldar, A. (2005) *Lords of the Land: The War Over Israel's Settlements in the Occupied
      Territories, 1967–2007.* New York, NY: Nation Books.

Zharkevich, I. (2009) 'A new way of being young in Nepal: The idea of Maoist youth and dreams
      of a new man.' *Studies in Nepali History and Society 14*, 1, 67–105.

Subject Index

Author Index